MW01679869

Hoop Tales:

Tennessee Volunteers Men's Basketball

Randy Moore

INSIDERS' GUIDE®

GUILFORD, CONNECTICUT

AN IMPRINT OF THE GLOBE PEQUOT PRESS

To buy books in quantity for corporate use
or incentives, call **(800) 962–0973, ext. 4551,**
or e-mail **premiums@GlobePequot.com.**

INSIDERS' GUIDE®

Copyright © 2005 by The Globe Pequot Press

All rights reserved. No part of this book may be reproduced or transmitted in any form by any means, electronic or mechanical, including photocopying and recording, or by any information storage and retrieval system, except as may be expressly permitted by the 1976 Copyright Act or by the publisher. Requests for permission should be made in writing to The Globe Pequot Press, P.O. Box 480, Guilford, Connecticut 06437.

Insiders' Guide is a registered trademark of The Globe Pequot Press.
Hoop Tales is a trademark of Morris Book Publishing, LLC.

Text design: Casey Shain
All photos are courtesy of the University of Tennessee Sports Information Department.
Cover photos: *front cover:* Ron Slay; *back cover:* top, Harry Anderson; bottom, Allan Houston.

Library of Congress Cataloging-in-Publication Data
Moore, Randy, 1952-
Hoop tales : Tennessee Volunteers men's basketball / Randy Moore.
p. cm. — (Hoop tales series)
ISBN 0-7627-3702-6
1. University of Tennessee, Knoxville—Basketball. 2. Tennessee Volunteers (Basketball team) I. Title: Tennessee Volunteers men's basketball. II. Title. III. Series.

GV885.43.U58M66 2005
796.323'63'0976885—dc22 2005043449

Manufactured in the United States of America
First Edition/First Printing

For my father, a diehard Volunteer fan, if ever there was one.

Contents

Acknowledgments

Special thanks to Bud Ford, Craig Pinkerton, and the rest of the UT Sports Information Department for their invaluable assistance.

Prologue

Eighteen years after James Naismith tossed a soccer ball through a bottomless peach basket nailed to the rafters of the YMCA gym in Springfield, Massachusetts, the new game called basketball made its intercollegiate debut on the University of Tennessee campus.

The date was December 16, 1909, and a capacity crowd of roughly 200 people jammed into the cozy YMCA gymnasium on The Hill, eagerly anticipating an eight o'clock tip-off between the Volunteers and Kentucky Central (now Centre College).

Because the train carrying the visitors was late, the game's start was postponed by more than an hour. To fill the dead time, a hastily assembled group of female students was paired against Knoxville's Central High School girls' team. The well-prepared high schoolers romped 21–1.

Fortunately for the assembled spectators, the varsity game that followed was considerably more competitive. Although the *Knoxville Journal and Tribune* noted the visitors' starting five included three "great strapping fellows," Tennessee's quickness and home-floor advantage kept the game close. In fact, the competition was so intense and the lead changes so frequent that the *Journal and Tribune* reported fans spent the evening on "the anxious bench" as "the interest was kept at the highest pitch."

Ultimately, Tennessee got just enough points from its starting five—led by forward Howard Sandberg with 13—to prevail 33–31.

And that's how it all began.

Nowhere to Go but Up

The 1927–28 school year was a memorable one in University of Tennessee athletics. A 7–7 tie with Kentucky was the only blemish in a stellar 8–0–1 Volunteer football season. Whereas the gridiron team approached perfection, the basketball team actually achieved it—albeit in a futile sense—by going 0–12.

Head coach William H. "Bill" Britton was disappointed but not surprised. He knew progress would be slow when the job was thrust upon him the previous year.

Determined to be the first man in school history to coach exclusively football, Robert R. Neyland took the gridiron reins in 1926 and immediately designated assistant coach Britton to oversee the basketball program. Britton's qualifications were a bit suspect; he had played the sport at West Point but had never coached above the church-league level. This, of course, was of absolutely no concern to Neyland.

"He always managed to push jobs off on me that he didn"t want," Britton quipped.

Neyland's lack of respect for Tennessee's basketball program was understandable. Except for a 12–0 season in 1915–16 and 15–2 seasons in 1913–14 and 1922–23, Volunteer hoops had been mired in mediocrity for most of its first two decades. And there was no reason to suspect 1926–27 would be any different.

Upon holding his first practice in October 1926, Britton was chagrined when "five or six skinny little kids showed up." Worse, only two of them had ever played college basketball. The head man was not encouraged by the early practice sessions, but he was even less encouraged upon seeing his team in competition for the first time.

"When Knoxville High School beat us in a scrimmage game," he noted, "I knew we had a couple of hard years ahead."

He was right. The 1926–27 team opened with a 23–20 home-court loss to Tennessee Wesleyan and eventually closed with a 7–12 record. In between, the Volunteers managed to lose twice each to Maryville College and Carson Newman.

It seemed highly unlikely that 1927–28 could be worse but it was. Much worse, in fact. Clearly exhibiting which sport was king of The Hill, team captain Elvin Butcher missed preseason basketball drills to play in an all-star football game on the West Coast. Predictably, the hoops season went downhill from there.

As happened a year earlier, the 1927–28 season opened with a loss to Tennessee Wesleyan. This time, though, things got worse instead of better. The Volunteers fell 25–20 to Maryville College, then suffered a 63–14 humiliation at the hands of Auburn. After a 31–26 loss to Georgia Tech, they endured successive blowout losses to Alabama (45–22); Georgetown, Kentucky (52–18); Kentucky (48–18); Louisville (49–29); Kentucky (43–16); and Georgia Tech (42–25).

Tennessee competed a little better in a 39–31 loss to Sewanee and entered the season finale with about as much confidence as an 0–11 team could muster. The Volunteers played Vanderbilt tough that day, but a late basket gave the Commodores a 28–26 triumph, mercifully ending the first winless season in the history of Tennessee's program.

With nowhere to go but up, Britton knew he needed help and knew where he could find it. Respectfully approaching his boss, he asked Neyland for some football players to pad his roster. He specifically requested Bobby Dodd, who had played some roundball in high school.

"Dodd is skinny as a rail," Neyland grumbled. "He kicks wobbly punts and throws wobbly passes, and he's as slow as molasses."

Still Dodd was better than anyone on the basketball roster, which he proved by starting at guard for three years and serving as team captain in year two. Britton also lured Gene McEver and

Though "skinny as a rail" and "slow as molasses," Bobby Dodd starred in basketball and football.

Buddy Hackman off the football team. Though considerably less skilled than Dodd, they were physically imposing "policemen" who excelled at the rough-and-tumble play of the era.

"I remember sending those two guys into a game down at Chattanooga," Britton recalled. "We were behind and were just getting whipped something awful, physically. It didn't take McEver and Hackman very long to just about wipe the whole place out. After we got ahead, I took them out because I didn't want anyone to get hurt. The way it turned out, I should have left them in because Chattanooga came back and won the ball game!"

McEver was particularly adept at the physical aspect of 1920s basketball. Nicknamed "Wild Bull" for his hard-nosed running style, he was cited by the *Knoxville Journal* following a game with Maryville College for "knocking down seven opposing players and twice squeezed the air out of the ball."

Another football player who proved to be an enforcer on the hardwood was tackle Bob "Oscar" Stafford. Britton termed him "just about the toughest man I've ever seen in a basketball uniform," adding, "He could handle anybody physically."

Stafford proved as much in a 1931 game at Georgia. He wore out two Bulldog centers—including All-South football player "Catfish" Smith—before fouling out himself. Stafford then celebrated in the shower by repeatedly shouting, "I can whip any damned man who ever played center for Georgia!"

Britton also pried gridders Paul Hug, Hugh Faust, Hugo Thayer, Beattie Feathers, and Breezy Wynn from Neyland's grasp—once football season had concluded, of course.

In time, Britton found fertile recruiting ground in his own backyard. Knoxville High School provided him with such quality players as Claude Reeder, Polk Crumbliss, Red Kirk, and Ernie O'Conner. Buoyed by the footballers and the homegrown heroes, Britton's program made a dramatic turnaround. Following the 0–12 disaster of 1927–28, his remaining teams combined to go 73–48.

The 1934–35 team—led by Harry Anderson, Biggy Marshall, and Gene Johnson—went 10–5 and pushed powerful Kentucky to the limit before bowing 38–36. With all five starters returning for 1935–36, Britton clearly had the Volunteers poised on the brink of greatness. When Neyland was called to military duty in Panama, however, Britton agreed to give up the hoops job in order to serve as interim football coach.

A. Watt Hobt, who helped with the football and basketball programs during those days, told Britton, "You're a darned fool to leave a basketball team that's going to be as good as this one."

Whether he was foolish or not is debatable, but Britton clearly was loyal.

"I had no choice," he said of the switch. "I felt that I owed it to the school to try and hold the football situation together."

By the time Neyland returned from Panama, the basketball program was in the capable hands of Blair Gullion, and the football program was poised for the unbeaten regular seasons of 1938, 1939, and 1940.

Gullion had played under the respected Ward "Piggy" Lambert at Purdue in the 1920s, had coached at Earlham (Indiana) College, and had authored several books on basketball techniques. A stickler for discipline, Gullion insisted his team run set plays. As Biggy Marshall recalled years later, "If they didn't work the first time, we took the ball back out to the guards, set back up, and ran them again."

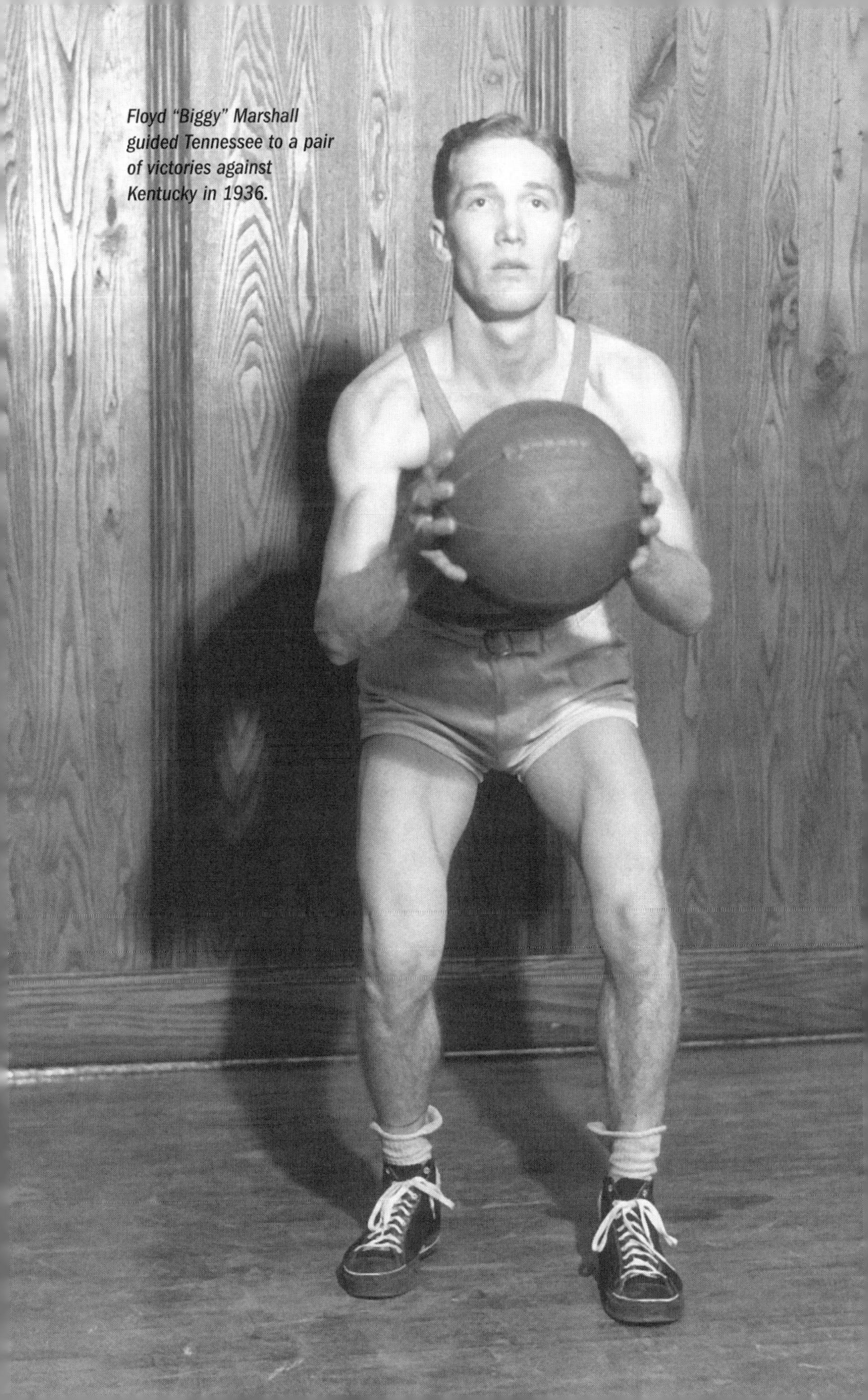

Floyd "Biggy" Marshall guided Tennessee to a pair of victories against Kentucky in 1936.

"There Was Only One Ref"

A personal foul, like beauty, is in the eye of the beholder. No one knew that better than rugged Harry Anderson, who in 1935–36 became Tennessee's first All-America basketball player. Although he averaged 14 points per game, the 6'4" Anderson was much better at preventing points than scoring them. In the 1936 Southeastern Conference Tournament, for instance, he limited three opposing centers to a combined total of 4 points. "Things would get pretty rough under the boards in those days," he explained, "but there was only one ref and he couldn't see everything."

Signed to a track scholarship following a standout career at Messick High School in Memphis, Anderson distinguished himself by breaking Tennessee's school records in the 100-yard dash (9.5 seconds), 220-yard dash (21.7 seconds), long jump (23 feet, 8 inches), and high jump (6 feet, 1 inch). He also ran on a couple of relay units.

Although track and basketball kept him pretty busy, Anderson once decided to try out for the Volunteer football team. It was to be a short-lived venture. That was because head basketball coach Bill Britton also served as an assistant for Bob Neyland's Volunteer football team.

Anderson showed up for football practice one day, only to be spotted by his basketball coach. What happened next was predictable. In Anderson's words, "Britton chased me off."

Harry Anderson played it rough under the boards.

Consecutive losses to Xavier, Kentucky, and Georgia—all on the road—dropped Tennessee's record to 6–5 late in the 1935–36 season. Game by game, though, the team was becoming accustomed to Gullion's methodical style of play. After beating Alabama 28–20, the Volunteers avenged the earlier loss to Kentucky by trouncing the Wildcats 39–28 in Knoxville. Marshall led the scoring with 17 points.

Following a 33–30 loss at Vanderbilt, Tennessee won its next three games to finish the regular season with an 11–6 record. Since two-year-old Alumni Memorial Gym was the Southeastern Conference's newest facility, Tennessee was picked to host the league tournament. Exploiting this home-court advantage, the Volunteers beat Auburn 43–25 in round one, then clipped Kentucky in round two. As in the regular-season meeting with the Big Blue, Marshall again paced Tennessee with 17 points. And, oddly enough, the final score was once again 39–28.

Perhaps nervous about playing for the league championship in front of their home crowd, the Volunteers scored just 4 points in the first eighteen minutes of the title game against Alabama. With his team down 13–4 and two minutes left in the first half, however, Anderson came to the rescue. The rules of the day called for a center jump after each made basket, rather than alternating possessions, and Tennessee exploited this to full advantage. Anderson, a 6'4" center with remarkable timing and jumping ability, got every tip the remainder of the half, enabling the Volunteers to pull within 13–11 by the intermission. Building on that momentum, Tennessee continued to play well in the second half. By the final horn, the Volunteers had a 29–25 victory and the first conference championship in program history.

Gullion's second team was almost as successful, going 15–4 in regular- season play and reaching the 1937 league title game before bowing 39–25 to Kentucky. His third team went a respectable 15–8, then lost in the 1938 tournament semifinals 45–40 to Ole Miss.

Despite an outstanding 47–19 record, Gullion mysteriously bolted Tennessee mere weeks before the 1938–39 season was to begin, accepting the reins at Cornell. Reportedly he and Major Neyland (who was also the athletics director by this time) did not see eye-to-eye on some key issues. Even with a .712 winning percentage, Gullion could never win that confrontation.

Still, his three years on The Hill saw him produce Tennessee's first conference championship and lay the groundwork for a second.

0:01

Mauer Matches Up with Rupp

Practice lasted a little longer. The drills grew a little tougher. The coach's mood became a little gruffer. Without checking the schedule, Tennessee's players of the late 1930s and early 1940s knew who the next opponent was . . . the University of Kentucky Wildcats.

Facing the Big Blue was more than special for Volunteer head man John Mauer; it was personal. He had guided Kentucky's program from 1928–30, recording an imposing 40–14 record and .740 winning percentage that dwarfed the 3–13 and .187 marks of predecessor Basil Hayden. On the heels of a spectacular 16–3 season in 1929–30, however, the school brass at Kentucky showed Mauer the door while flinging it open for a young upstart named Adolph Rupp.

Mauer exited quietly but grudgingly, and he carried that grudge to his grave. That's why he left a successful program at Miami of Ohio two months before the start of the 1938–39 season to accept the reins at Tennessee. Coaching the Volunteers would give Mauer at least two opportunities per season to meet—and defeat—the man Kentucky had hired to replace him.

"Mauer and Rupp didn't like each other," recalls Bill Wright, a starting guard during Mauer's Tennessee tenure. "Mauer was upset when Kentucky let him go and hired Rupp, and the two of them never did get along well. You could tell from the way Mauer talked that he didn't care too much for Rupp."

Mauer's first opportunity to upstage his successor did not look promising. The 1938–39 Volunteers were 6–2 overall but 0–2 in Southeastern Conference play following road losses at Alabama and Mississippi State. Clearly, this was a bad time to face Kentucky in Lexington. Then again, there is no good time to face Kentucky in Lexington.

Perhaps the Wildcats overlooked the struggling Volunteers. Perhaps Tennessee's players relaxed due to the seeming futility of the task before them. Perhaps all of the planets in the universe were aligned just right. Perhaps Mauer's desire for vengeance superceded Kentucky's superior personnel. Whatever the reason, the Volunteers stunned the Wildcats literally—and the rest of the college basketball world figuratively—by winning 30–29 on that fateful day.

"That one gave us a big lift," Mauer noted. "From that time on, everyone connected with the basketball program was sold on it and felt we could compete, and win, against the best."

The best, of course, was Kentucky. Rupp had guided the Wildcats to the top rung on college basketball's ladder, and nothing thrilled Mauer more than knocking them from that lofty perch, even temporarily.

"Coach Mauer always had pretty good success against Kentucky," Wright said. "He always got pumped up for that game, and so did we. They were the big wheel in the conference and usually won the league championship. We always had extra preparation and harder practices the week before a Kentucky game."

Whatever Mauer did to prepare for the Wildcats, it worked. In an era when Rupp crushed most of his contemporaries, Mauer proved to be a real test for the Baron of the Bluegrass. He went 1–2 vs. Rupp in 1939 (winning 30–29 in Lexington, losing 38–36 in Knoxville, and falling 46–38 in the league tournament). He went 1–2 again in 1940 (winning 27–23 in Knoxville, losing 35–26 in Lexington, and bowing 30–29 in the conference tournament). He went 2–1 in 1941 (prevailing 32–22 in Knoxville and 36–33 in the league tourney, but losing 37–28 in Lexington). He split two games in 1942 (winning 46–40 in Knoxville, losing 36–33 in Lexington).

Rupp won both regular-season meetings in 1943, but Mauer got revenge in the Southeastern Conference championship game that March, winning 33–30. After World War II wiped out the 1944 season, Mauer and Rupp were at it again in 1945. Mauer won 35–34 at Knoxville in January, improving his head-to-head record against Rupp to 7–8. At this point the Baron finally took control of the rivalry, winning the remaining six meetings to finish with a 14–7 advantage.

Although beating Kentucky was personal for Mauer, it was just as fulfilling for his players.

"It was just something you knew you'd remember for your lifetime," Wright recalls. "And it was something that didn't happen too often."

In addition to his basketball duties, Mauer was the head baseball coach at Tennessee and also an assistant football coach. He was so highly regarded in the last endeavor that he had to attend preparations for the 1944 Rose Bowl game with the University of Southern California, leaving Maryville College's Lombe Honaker to coach the Volunteer basketball team in a high-profile game with New York University at Madison Square Garden.

Mauer's success in athletics was almost inevitable. He competed with and against several of the premier athletes and coaches of the twentieth century, and some of their magic may have rubbed off on him. He was a teammate of football immortal Red Grange at the University of Illinois. He served as a football aide to Red Blaik at West Point, where he became good friends with fellow Cadet assistant and future Green Bay Packer head coach Vince Lombardi. During his basketball coaching tenure at Miami of Ohio, Mauer's star player was Walter Alston, who subsequently spent two decades as manager of Major League Baseball's Los Angeles Dodgers. At Tennessee, Mauer coached with legendary Bob Neyland on the gridiron and against the equally legendary Rupp on the hardwood.

"Coach Mauer was a real gentleman from the old school," recalls Wright, who went on to distinguish himself as Tennessee's head baseball coach. "I liked him a lot and respected him. But he always had his game face on. He didn't put up with any nonsense, in practice or the games. Everything was serious."

As serious as Mauer was the rest of the time, his single-mindedness hit a new level whenever he squared off against the volatile Rupp. Tennessee fans hit a new level when Rupp came to town, as well.

"Adolph was up off the bench, yelling at the officials all the time," Wright said. "There was a rooting section in the balcony just above the visitor's' bench at Alumni Gym, and a lot of former Tennessee football players would sit up there and taunt Rupp—yelling at him to sit down and shut up, things like that."

The taunts weren't the only reason Adolph hated visiting Alumni Gym, though. The tiny building featured all the folksy charm of a dungeon.

"Rupp always complained about the lighting at Alumni Gym," Wright said. "I have to admit, it was pretty dim in there. The lights were way up in the ceiling and not very high wattage."

After complaining bitterly about the lighting for several years, Rupp decided to save his breath and state his case in another way. He smugly showed up for one game at Alumni wearing a light-beaming miner's helmet.

Mauer's glory years were 1940–41, 1941–42, and 1942–43. During that stretch he won fifty of sixty-two games, claiming league titles in 1941 and 1943. He posted one of the biggest victories in school history on December 30, 1941, knocking off topranked Long Island University 36–33 to snap LIU's twenty-three-game winning streak.

The star players during this time were Frank Thomas, Gilbert Huffman, and Bernie Mehen—a trio Mauer collectively referred to as "The Three Musketeers." Thomas was an under-

Bernie Mehen's showmanship earned him the nickname "Houdini."

sized center in the 6' 3", 180-pound range. Huffman was a 6'1" guard, and Mehen was a 6'4" forward nicknamed "Houdini" for his sleight-of-hand skills on the basketball floor.

"Bernie was a great showman," Wright recalls. "He had several tricks that might not be considered sensational today, but in those days they were. He loved to dribble between his legs and pass behind his back, things like that."

Mehen's favorite piece of showmanship was a variation of baseball's hidden-ball trick. Dribbling the ball in backcourt, he'd deftly catch it between his knees, and then swing his arm forward as if heaving a long pass to a wide-open teammate. Invariably the defender would leave Mehen's side and race down the floor. Invariably the crowd would erupt.

"That always brought down the house," Wright says.

Not surprisingly, Tennessee's fans found Mehen's colorful antics a lot more amusing than Tennessee's coach did.

"Mauer didn't like 'em very much," Wright recalls. "As a freshman Bernie was always throwing the ball behind his back and dribbling between his legs. Mauer calmed him down quite a bit when he joined the varsity. Mauer wasn't into showmanship; he just wanted to win."

That became abundantly clear in a 1941 game at Vanderbilt. With Tennessee nursing a 1-point lead in the final minute, Mehen disregarded Mauer's instructions to play conservatively and draw a foul. An ill-advised behind-the-back pass was intercepted and turned into a Commodore layup that gave the hosts a 1-point lead. Mehen would've been the goat except for a kiss from Lady Luck. Fouled while attempting a 40-foot desperation shot at the buzzer, he made two free throws after time had expired to give Tennessee a 37–36 victory.

As fate would have it, Mehen wound up sharing a cab with the still-smoldering Mauer on the ride back to the team hotel. After several uneasy minutes, Mehen finally broke the awkward silence.

"Coach," he said, "if I ever pull that stunt in a situation like that again, I wish you'd come out there and kick my butt in front of the whole crowd."

"Bernie," Mauer snapped, "you don't know how close I came to doing just that tonight!"

When he wasn't inciting his own coach, Mehen was inciting rival coaches. In the 1941 Southeastern Conference title game against Kentucky, he absolutely infuriated Rupp with an assortment of flashy tricks. Finally, he used his signature move—catching the ball between his knees, then faking a long pass. As a confused Wildcat defender searched frantically for the ball, Rupp leaped up from the Big Blue bench, pointed at Mehen's knees and snarled, "There it is, G— damn it!"

Mehen's magic act earned him two years of All-Southeastern Conference recognition and All-America honors as a senior. Moreover, he helped the Volunteers post a 50–15 record during his three-year career.

With Mehen out of eligibility, Tennessee projected to be an also-ran in the 1942–43 league race. The starting lineup that year consisted of Wright, Paul Herman, Dick Fromm, Ted Cook, and Dick Mehen, Bernie's younger brother.

Following a sizzling 10–1 start, the Volunteers slumped badly. They dropped three of their last four regular-season games, including a 53–29 annihilation at Lexington. After a first-round bye, however, Tennessee beat Vanderbilt (41–31) and Louisiana State University (52–34) in the league tournament. Bernie Mehen scored exactly half of the Volunteers points in the LSU

Dick Mehen (left) helped John Mauer's 1942–43 Volunteers capture the Southeastern Conference title.

game, helping Tennessee secure a berth in the title game. The opponent, of course, was Kentucky.

Mere weeks after losing by 24 points in Lexington, the Volunteers were given little chance of winning the rematch. But Mehen scored 18 points, and Cook held Big Blue ace Milt Ticco scoreless for the entire game, guiding Tennessee to a 33–30 victory. Wright remembers it well.

"The tournament was played in the Armory Fieldhouse at Louisville, and the crowd was all Kentucky," he said. "There probably weren't a dozen Tennessee people in the building. When they called us up to accept the trophy, there was a deathly silence in there. There wasn't a sound as they presented the trophy to Coach Mauer.

"That made us happy. We felt like we'd really hurt 'em."

There was no clamoring crowd of well-wishers cheering the victorious Volunteers upon their return to Knoxville. The players slipped back into town as quietly as they had departed.

"They didn't even broadcast the game in Knoxville," Wright recalled. "When we came back, nobody much said anything about it. There was a big article in the newspaper, but nobody much knew anything about it."

Despite the lack of fanfare, none of the Volunteers felt slighted.

"We figured we got as much publicity as we deserved," Wright said. "None of Tennessee's sports except football got much attention in those days, so we weren't concerned about it."

Still, with two conference titles in three years, the Volunteers were on a roll. Ultimately, their momentum would be stopped, not by Kentucky, but by World War II. The hostilities forced cancellation of the 1943–44 season.

When play resumed in 1944–45, Tennessee's program scarcely missed a beat. Paul "Lefty" Walther, a native of Covington, Kentucky, scored 21 points, as the Volunteers capped a 4–0 start by upsetting New York University 50–48 at Madison Square Garden. Tennessee split its regular-season meetings with Kentucky and won the regular-season conference title with a 15–3 record. The Big Blue prevailed 39–35 in the title game of the league tournament, but Tennessee's consolation prize was a first-ever bid to the National Invitation Tournament in New York City. The Volunteers bowed 51–44 to Rhode Island in round one, finishing 18–5.

Walther, who made several All-America teams as a seventeen-year-old freshman, would not be back for 1945–46. Now old enough to serve in the military, he left a gaping hole in the Volunteer lineup. Still, Tennessee went a respectable 15–7.

Walther returned for 1946–47—as did Dick Mehen, Cook, Wright, Marshall Hawkins, and Bill Bailey from the 1942–43 championship team—but the rest of the league was playing for second place that season. Kentucky's entire starting five of Ralph Beard, Alex Groza, Wallace "Wah Wah" Jones, Jack Tingle, and Joe Holland earned all-conference recognition as the Wildcats tuned up for a run that would see them win national titles in 1948, 1949, and 1951.

"They had a lot of players . . . more than they knew what to do with," Wright recalls. "They were loaded, but a lot of teams were loaded at that time. You had your new recruits, plus the guys who had played during the war *and* the guys back from the war.

"Kentucky had guys who had been All-Americans during the war who couldn't even make the team after the war. Wah Wah Jones didn't start either of the games they played against us that

"Lefty" Left His Mark

There is a common perception that left-handed athletes tend to be eccentrics, if not outright flakes. This belief may have begun with Paul Walther, a star basketball player for the Tennessee Volunteers in the 1940s.

Joining the program after a standout career at Xavier High School in Cincinnati, "Lefty" quickly proved as adept at showmanship as he was at basketball. Almost comically slender at 6'2" and 145 pounds, he would spend pregame warm-ups flipping the ball behind his back or between his legs. Sometimes he'd bounce it off his head or even kick it to a teammate.

Paul "Lefty" Walther

Lefty's zest for the zany sometimes overshadowed the fact he was a truly outstanding basketball player. He was the first Volunteer ever to score 400 points in a season, ringing up 462 as a senior. His 17.7-points-per-game average that year was the highest in school history to that time. Head coach Emmett Lowery once said of him, "Inch for inch and pound for pound, Lefty Walther was as fine a player as there was in college basketball in his day."

After college Walther distinguished himself in the National Basketball Association, earning all-star recognition in 1951 and 1952. He spent part of his career with Philadelphia, often playing doubleheaders with the colorful Harlem Globetrotters. He showed a few of his crowd-pleasing moves to the 'Trotters, who shared his zest for showmanship. "Just think," Walther once mused, "if it had happened a few years later, I might have been the first white Globetrotter in history."

year. In fact, he only played the last two minutes against us."

Wright's roommate in 1946–47 was Walther, whose knack for showmanship may have surpassed that of Tennessee predecessor Bernie Mehen.

"Lefty was quite a character," Wright recalled. "He clowned around a lot, but he was a real hypochondriac. He was always using nasal spray and taking throat lozenges. His dresser was covered with medications of every kind."

When he wasn't treating an assortment of aches and pains in the dormitory room, Walther was likely to be found on the basketball floor, inflicting aches and pains with his spindly elbows.

"He was a real skinny guy, and he had the sharpest elbows of anybody I ever knew," Wright said. "Everybody was always trying to stay away from his elbows in scrimmages, but he got me one time and cut my face."

An even more unpleasant aspect of the 1946–47 season occurred around Christmas time. Following a December 21 loss to Long Island University at Madison Square Garden, the Volunteers traveled to the Pittsburgh area for the next game of their road trip. Expecting to face Duquesne, they faced an angry mob instead.

Southeastern Conference policy of the time banned its schools from competing against teams that were racially integrated. Duquesne had a black freshman on its team, but the head coach had assured Mauer beforehand that the rookie would not play against the Volunteers.

"When we got to the gym, though, the black player was dressed out," Wright recalled. "There was a big hullabaloo about it, then Coach Mauer called all of us together to see if we wanted to play. Of course we all wanted to play. Most of us had played against black athletes in either high school or the service, so it didn't make any difference to us."

Perplexed, Mauer placed a long-distance telephone call to General Neyland, who doubled as Tennessee's athletics director. Neyland said the SEC's policy was clear and that Tennessee had to abide by it. The disappointed Volunteers returned to their dressing room and tugged on their street clothes.

"We thought it was kind of ridiculous," Wright recalls, "but there wasn't anything we could do about it."

Returning to the playing floor on their way to the exits, Tennessee's players found thousands of angry Duquesne fans waiting for them.

"We had to have a police escort to get out of the gym," Wright recalled. "People were yelling at us and cursing us. They may have thrown some stuff at us, but I got out of there so fast I can't say for sure. There were cabs waiting for us outside the gym, so we took them to the airport and got out of there before there was any more trouble."

Tennessee's head coach bore the brunt of the indignation that followed.

"Coach Mauer took a lot of flak and got a lot of telephone calls in the middle of the night," Wright recalled. "He was harassed a good bit because people thought he made the decision not to play that game. It was out of his hands, though. You did what the general said if you wanted to keep on coaching."

Three months later, following a second-round loss to Tulane in the 1947 SEC tournament, Mauer left Tennessee to take the reins at West Point. The man who came in with a roar had gone out with a whimper. Still, his legacy was secure. Mauer's eight-season reign produced two regular-season conference titles, two tournament titles, and a .755 winning percentage that ranks as the finest in program history to this day.

Oh, yeah. And he whipped Rupp seven times.

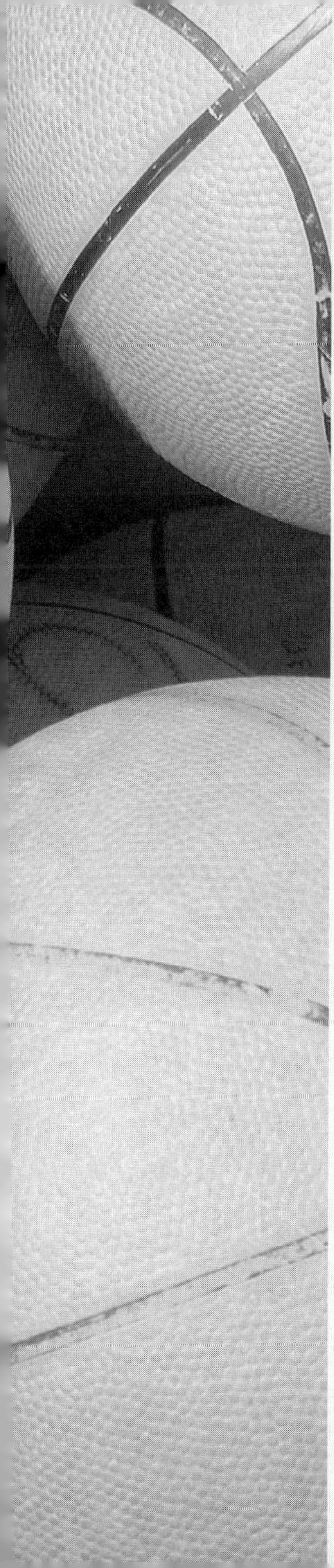

An Udder Rebounding Machine

He is, without question, the greatest rebounder in University of Tennessee basketball history. Long before he made his name by grabbing rebounds, though, Gene Tormohlen made his game by grabbing udders back in Holland, Indiana.

He was twelve years old when he got a job on an older cousin's farm, working the hay fields from dawn till dusk. His arms and back ached, but his day wasn't finished yet.

"My cousin and I would bale hay for around twelve hours each day," Tormohlen recalls. "Once it got too dark to work the fields, we would milk six or seven cows each. Anyone who has ever tried it knows: Milking cows strengthens your arms and hands."

At age sixteen he got a chance to move up in the milk-making process. No longer content squeezing udders, he landed a job collecting containers of fresh milk and delivering them to the local dairy. He toiled six days per week from 4:00 A.M. until noon, yet the new job seemed like a holiday compared to farming. "I was working eight hours a day instead of twelve," he says, "and I was getting about five times the pay I was before."

Still, the new job was plenty arduous. Milk was stored in ten-gallon steel containers, and young Tormohlen had to visit dozens of local farms each morning, load the heavy containers onto a truck, then unload them upon arriving at the factory. "The cans weighed probably one hundred pounds each," he recalls. "You didn't have to carry them far, but it was a tiring job that wasn't made for sissies. Those things would get pretty heavy by the end of the day."

The taxing work made Tormohlen awfully tired, but it also made him a great basketball player. The powerful shoulder and back muscles he developed while toting milk cans would help him years later when he was jockeying for position under the backboards. The bulging forearms and viselike grip he developed during his cow-milking days would enable him to clamp down on virtually every rebound he touched. He didn't realize it at the time, but those summer jobs essentially amounted to an off-season conditioning program. "We didn't lift weights in those days, but working on that milk truck every summer was almost like lifting weights," Tormohlen recalls. "I think that made me a little stronger than the average bear that came down the creek. Then I used that strength to hit the boards."

Indeed he did. Dalen Showalter, a Volunteer teammate during Tormohlen's junior and senior seasons, remembers Big Gene as "the strongest man I ever knew." Tormohlen's size and strength might have been wasted, though, if not for his all-out tenacity. "Personally, he was always a very nice and kind and gentle man," Showalter says. "But when he got in a ball game, he was mean. He went after the ball no matter who was in his way—Tennessee players . . . opposing players . . . it didn't matter. He just wanted the ball.

"Gene wasn't a great jumper, but he was strong, and he went to the glass really hard. He was just a fantastic rebounder."

In addition to size, strength, and determination, Tormohlen was blessed with another attribute that made him a truly dominating rebounder: He had a sixth sense for reading the ball's flight and anticipating its eventual destination. "There's a certain knack to rebounding," he says. "I used technique. I positioned myself properly and studied the flight of the ball in anticipation of where it would bounce off the backboard or rim. You have to read the ball."

Finally there was his abundant confidence. A lot of guys try to get every rebound, but Tormohlen *expected* to get every rebound. "My high school coach told me when the ball is shot, go for every rebound as if the ball is yours," he recalled. "Very few guys do that, but I always did. I enjoyed rebounding, and there were nights when I thought I was getting all of them."

One of those nights was February 11, 1956, when he grabbed 27 rebounds in a loss to Mississippi State. Another came in a 1957 game against Ole Miss, when he pulled down 31 rebounds and set a school record that stands to this day. Tormohlen's backboard prowess peaked during his senior year of 1958–59, when he ranked second nationally in rebounds per game. For his career, he grabbed 22 or more in a game a mind-boggling sixteen times.

Still, the greatest testament to Tormohlen's skills as a backboard crasher is this: Nearly half a century after he played his final college game, he still ranks 1–2–3 on the school's single-season rebounding list—averaging 17.7 per game in 1958–59, 16.7 in 1957–58, and 16.2 in 1956–57. His career average of 16.9 per game far outdistances runner-up Bernard King, who averaged 13.2 for the Vols from 1974–77. "I knew I had a pretty good record," Tormohlen said in 2004, pausing before modestly adding, "but we didn't shoot as good as they do today, so there were more rebounds coming off."

All modesty aside, Tormohlen's signing by Tennessee headman Emmett Lowery in 1956 represented a turning point in Volunteer basketball history. In his first nine years on The Hill, Lowery's tallest starter was 6'6" Doug Atkins, who played just one season of hoops before concentrating on football. "By this time basketball was getting pretty commercial, and a lot of coaches were buying players on the open market, especially big men," Lowery once said. "After it became obvious that we needed more height very critically, a strong supporter of the university sports program came to me and said, 'Here's five thousand dollars. Go out and get yourself the best big man you can find.'

"I have to admit that I was tempted. It's not easy to get beat by teams that you know are doing that sort of thing, and I had as much pride as anyone else. But I had to tell him no. I realized that I was giving up a chance to get some extraordinary players, but I had to live with myself."

Sines Was Good with Lines

John Sines wasn't the sharpest coach in Vol basketball history, but he may have had the sharpest wit. Elevated from assistant coach to head man when Emmett Lowery retired, Sines lasted just three seasons—posting records of 12–11, 10–15, and 4–19 from 1959–62. Although he didn't produce many victories, he certainly provided two of the greatest wisecracks in program history.

The first came in the 1950s, when he was still assisting Lowery. The calls were not going Tennessee's way in a game against Vanderbilt, so Sines spent much of the evening peppering the officials with stinging insults. Finally, after a particularly cutting salvo from Sines, the nearest official turned to the scorer's table and called a technical foul on the Vol aide. Still, Sines got the last word. "That," he snapped, "is the first one you've called right all night!"

Sines's sense of humor had a dry side, too. Perhaps his greatest quip followed his greatest triumph. Moments after Tennessee completed a stunning 65–63 upset of Kentucky in the 1959—60 season finale at Lexington, the coach was hoisted onto his players' shoulders and carried from the court.

Afterward, Sines hinted the impromptu salute was more unsettling than flattering. "We never had practiced that," he deadpanned, "and they didn't know how to do it."

Not long after, Lowery and Vol aide John Sines discovered Tormohlen, then a rawboned sophomore at Holland (Indiana) High School. "Gene's talent was raw, but he had it," Lowery said. "Sines saw him win a high school tournament game by driving in and stuffing it two-handed in the last second of play and was sold on him from then on."

Tormohlen had everything Lowery was looking for—height, agility, strength, and toughness. Best of all, there was no price tag attached. The young giant wasn't interested in selling himself to the highest bidder. "Some schools offered me things—Tennessee didn't—but it was nickel-and-dime stuff compared to what goes on today," Tormohlen recalls. "There's always been a premium on big people, and there always will be."

That a guy from a basketball hotbed such as Indiana would slip out of state to Tennessee seems implausible. In truth it was implausible. But it happened anyway. "Everybody recruited me," Tormohlen says, "but Tennessee recruited my parents. Right there was the difference. Emmett did the job on my parents, and they wanted me to go to Tennessee. I really didn't care where I went. I'd never done anything for my parents in my life, so I thought I'd give it a whirl.

"If I had it to do over again—being a poor kid from a small community—I might stay closer to home. It was difficult being at Tennessee for nine months of the year, especially when you didn't have a car to go to the movies or anything. That was tough."

But Tormohlen was tough, too. In fact, he was a little too tough. He played with the ferocity of a Brahma bull . . . and with a similar level of finesse. "As a freshman he would flail away under the basket, fouling everybody in sight," Lowery said. "But he was an awfully good boy, and he smoothed out tremendously in his last two years."

Before he "smoothed out," however, Tormohlen was immensely entertaining to watch. Once, while scouting Butler University, Sines noticed that the team's center was a good driver but poor shooter. Returning to Knoxville, he instructed Tormohlen to ignore shooting fakes and play the drive. Apparently the towering Volunteer found the advice difficult to follow. "Well, the first time the guy faked, Big Gene jumped clear out of the gym, and he just dribbled in and laid it in," Lowery recalled. "It went that way all night."

Tormohlen's penchant for fouling may have cost Tennessee a colossal upset victory on December 29, 1958. With ten minutes left and Tennessee leading fifth-ranked West Virginia, Tormohlen picked up foul number five and took a seat on the Vol bench. The Mountaineers, thanks to 44 points from Jerry West, rallied to win 76–72.

"I told Jerry West they never would've won if I hadn't fouled out," Tormohlen recalls with a laugh. "He got 44 against us that night, so I'd say he was pretty good. I'd seen Oscar Robertson play in high school, then I saw Jerry play in college. I knew then they were both going to be awfully good, but I had no idea they'd be two of the top guards that ever played the game."

Tormohlen and Robertson never faced one another in high school, but they came close once. Holland High was ranked number seventeen heading into the 1955 Indiana state tournament, while Robertson and Crispus Attucks High were ranked number one. Tormohlen and company shocked third-ranked Jasper in a first-round game he recalls as "the most fun I ever had in high school," but Holland was eliminated before it could face Robertson's team. In retrospect, that may have been a blessing. "We thought we could compete with Crispus Attucks,"

His Fouls Weren't Personal

No one in University of Tennessee basketball history ever grabbed more rebounds. Likewise no one in Volunteer annals ever committed more fouls. If there was anything Gene Tormohlen did with greater gusto than hit the backboards, it was hit opponents. It wasn't intentional; it was just a natural by-product of his rough-and-tumble playing style.

"He fouls a lot," Volunteer head man Emmett Lowery once said. "But his fouls are motivated by his great desire to win. He sees a loose ball and goes for it. When a fast break develops, he's running harder than anybody. He'll get under one basket and jump and jump, then run 90 feet and jump some more."

This lofty level of determination earned Tormohlen a lot of fouls but also a lot of respect. Of course, Lowery knew better than anyone how special Tormohlen was. "He can go longer and play harder than any man his size I've ever seen," Tennessee's head coach said. "When he doesn't have foul trouble, he can go the full game at pretty much top speed."

The key phrase, of course, was "When he doesn't have foul trouble . . ." Those times were rare. Tormohlen collected fouls the way some people collect stamps. Although he grabbed rebounds at a mind-numbing clip, he would've grabbed hundreds more if he hadn't spent so much time on the bench in foul trouble.

One quote from Lowery said it all: "He's a great favorite with the rest of the boys and they pull for him. . . . He pulls for them, too. I know, because I'm sitting beside him on the bench too much of the time."

Gene Tormohlen, Tennessee's undisputed rebounding king.

Tormohlen says. "But after I got to the NBA and found out just how good Oscar was, I was glad we hadn't faced them."

As the movie *Hoosiers* dramatically illustrated, Indiana high school basketball of the 1940s and 1950s might not have produced the most talent in America, but it produced the most passion. Prep hoops wasn't just a game; it was a happening that consumed entire communities. "Indiana people were crazy about basketball," Tormohlen recalls. "During the sectional, they'd close the town down. The stores closed, the service stations closed, and they only kept one or two cops around to make sure people didn't start looting everything."

Although he was bigger and stronger than most of his classmates, Tormohlen insists he wasn't much of a basketball player in his early high school days. "As a sophomore I was a 6'4" guard—the fifth man on the team, and lucky to be there," he recalls, adding with a laugh: "If anybody hit 2 shots in a row they took my spot. But the coach saw that I had potential."

Like many tall teenagers, Tormohlen was a late bloomer. Once his coordination caught up with his size, he quickly evolved into a force on the basketball floor. "When I was a senior I really tore loose," he says. "I got to believing I was pretty good, and I believed that for a long time."

Going from basketball-crazy Indiana to football-crazy Knoxville represented quite a culture shock. The first time he saw 3,200-seat Alumni Memorial Gym, Tormohlen figured there must be some sort of mistake. "Their little cracker-box gym was just a little better than what we had in high school," he says. "They promised that they'd build a new gym, though, and they did. They opened the Armory Fieldhouse (7,000-seat capacity) in time for my junior year."

Although he had dominated at the high school level back in Indiana, Tormohlen was unsure how he'd fare against the college boys at Tennessee. He found out in short order. "I believed I was good, but you never know until you get on the floor with those guys," he says. "About fifteen minutes into a pickup game before our first practice, I realized I belonged."

Many of Tennessee's better athletes of the era played both basketball and football. Tormohlen decided early on that he didn't want to be one of them. Although Bob Neyland had moved from head football coach to athletics director by this time, practices on the gridiron were still terribly intense and grueling. "I used to watch Tennessee's football scrimmages," Tormohlen recalls, "and it made me very thankful I was a basketball player."

Even at a school where football was king, Tormohlen's basketball exploits inspired some legendary tales. A few of them, he hints, were even true. For instance, he was so determined to help Tennessee snap a six-game losing streak against cross-state rival Vanderbilt that he suited up for a January 4, 1958, game in Knoxville despite an eight-stitch gash on his shooting hand. Playing through the pain, he scored 15 points and speared 17 rebounds as the Vols prevailed 67–55.

Later that season he reportedly committed two blocking fouls in a game at Kentucky, each time injuring the victimized Wildcat so severely that play had to be stopped and first-aid administered. Tormohlen is skeptical about the first-aid angle but says the part about the two blocking fouls is probably correct. "The Baron had control of everything," he recalls, referring to Kentucky coach Adolph Rupp. "They had me in foul trouble during the [pregame] warm-ups."

Ironically the same aggressive nature that made Tormohlen foul-prone as a collegian also made him the most successful rebounder of his era. Nobody did it better. "It was just my specialty," he says. "It's what got me there. I learned to shoot a little and pass a little after college. But rebounding got me in the door."

Tormohlen took justifiable pride in his backboard work. Grabbing the ball as it came off the rim was just as rewarding to him as swishing the net from 20 feet was to his teammates. "I'd just as soon get a rebound as score a basket," he says. "Rebounding is one statistic you can be selfish about. If you say to yourself, 'I'm going to be a great rebounder, you're helping your team. But if you say, 'I'm going to be a great scorer,' you're probably going to take some bad shots."

As dominating as he was on the backboards, Tormohlen was consistently overshadowed by another Southeastern Conference big man. "Bailey Howell was the best player in the conference," Tormohlen recalls. "He was 6'9" and played high post for Mississippi State. They'd throw it to him, and he'd take me one-on-one. I usually fouled out with four or five minutes left. I couldn't cover him then, couldn't cover him in the NBA, and I couldn't cover him now."

His futility against Howell notwithstanding, Tormohlen remembers his time on The Hill with great fondness. He and his teammates formed a bond during those days that continues with annual reunions to this day. Showalter believes the closeness of that team was forged in the dormitory. "All of the scholarship athletes stayed in East Stadium Dormitory except basketball," he says. "We had a section in South Stadium Dormitory at that time. We were a close-knit group, and that might explain why we formed such a tight bond."

That bond was never tighter than in the opening weeks of the 1958–59 season. Venturing north of the Mason-Dixon Line to play in the Midwestern Invitational at Kent, Ohio, the Volunteers encountered frigid conditions outside the gymnasium but little resistance inside it. Tennessee trounced Michigan (80–66) and Wyoming (90–69) to win the title with ease. "Probably the highlight of my college career was when we went up there and won that tournament in ten-below-zero weather," Tormohlen recalls. "Some of the guys didn't know it got that cold."

Being from Indiana, Tormohlen and Showalter were accustomed to blustery conditions and felt right at home in them. Conversely, some of their Southern-born teammates were panic-stricken at the sight of a few snowflakes. "My freshman year at Tennessee, we got an inch and a half of snow, and they canceled school for three days," Tormohlen recalls with a laugh. "Back in Indiana it wasn't uncommon to get 10 to 12 inches at one time."

Winning the Midwestern Invitational earned the Volunteers some national attention. They checked in at number six in the season's first Associated Press poll—the highest national ranking in program history. After beating Wake Forest to complete a 4–0 start, they edged up to number five. Suddenly Tennessee basketball was on the map, thanks to a couple of transplanted Hoosiers named Tormohlen and Showalter.

"Dalen was probably our best player," Tormohlen says. "He had a lot of character and was just a nickel's worth from being good enough to play in the NBA at that time. He'd make it today because there are so many more teams and so many more jobs. And Herman Thompson was the guy we looked up to for advice. Herman and Dalen were awfully special to Volunteer basketball during those days.

"All of the guys were special in one way or another, though. My senior year we didn't have a bad egg on the team. Emmett didn't get the best players in the world, but he got good people."

Ultimately, the 1958–59 Volunteers were better people than basketball players. They slumped badly once league action began. The team stood 13–7 overall and 7–5 in Southeastern Conference play heading into the final two regular-season games. The opponents were imposing—second-ranked Auburn and top-ranked Kentucky—but both games were in Knoxville, so the Volunteers were optimistic.

That optimism proved to be well-founded. Tennessee led Auburn in the second half and appeared on its way to a rousing victory. Then the unthinkable happened. Tormohlen was aggressively taking the ball to the basket when he was undercut by Auburn's Rex Frederick. After somersaulting in midair, Tormohlen landed on his head with a sickening thud and then went into convulsions.

Nearly fifty years later, Showalter still recalled that spill as "the hardest hit I've ever seen on a basketball floor," adding, "Rex Frederick didn't intentionally undercut him, but he went under him and sent him straight up and down. Gene landed on the floor and shook for a while. We were all concerned. The first thing that runs through your mind is, 'My God, he might die!' because he really crashed down on his head."

Tormohlen was rushed by ambulance to a Knoxville hospital, where he was diagnosed with a severe concussion. Understandably his recollections of the incident are a bit hazy. "I remember going to the basket and Frederick upsetting me," he says. "The next thing I heard was the siren on the way to the hospital. It still bothers me, to tell the truth. Forty years later a doctor showed me an X-ray of my head, and you could still see the damage I suffered in that fall."

After playing in sixty-six consecutive college games, Tormohlen hoped to go out with a bang in the finale against Kentucky. Someone at Tennessee even designed a soft helmet to protect his damaged head and reduce the risk of re-injury. "I don't know who came up with the helmet," he says, "but a doctor told me I shouldn't play even *with* the helmet. He said, 'If you fall on that same spot, you'll never get up again.'"

Despite the ominous warning, Tormohlen agonized as he pondered his options. In the end he decided to take the doctor's advice. "I finally told 'em no. If we were going for the SEC championship, I'd wear it and play. Since there's no championship at stake, I'll pass," he recalls. "I was a big country boy, and I didn't have anybody to advise me, so I tried to use the best common sense I could. I think it was a wise decision. I had nothing to prove, and our team couldn't prove anything more than it already had."

Although the Vols had held on to beat Auburn 56–55 following Tormohlen's injury, they were no match for Kentucky without the guy known as "Big Gene." Tennessee fell 77–66 in what proved to be the final game for both Tormohlen and head coach Emmett Lowery.

"Coach Lowery was a fine man but a terrible driver," Tormohlen says. "He'd go 60 miles an hour, then he'd go 40. He drove me crazy. I rode with him after we won the Midwestern Invitational championship, and that was the only bad part of the trip."

Tormohlen's next "trip" would be the professional ranks. Originally selected by Syracuse in round two of the National Basketball Association draft, he failed to make the team. He persevered, however, and two years later caught on with the St.

Emmett Lowery (below) finally got the big man he needed when Gene Tormohlen signed with Tennessee.

Louis Hawks. "There were only eight teams in the NBA then, so there were less than a hundred players in the league," he recalls. "I was fortunate to be one of them.

"The first time I put on a Hawks uniform and started out onto the floor, Lenny Wilkins was in front of me, Cliff Hagan on one side, and Bob Pettit on the other—three all-pros. I looked up at the sky and said, 'Lord, are you sure you want *me* out here with these guys?'"

Pro basketball was still in its infancy in those days, and there were growing pains galore. Tormohlen discovered as much in his first preseason with the Hawks. "One day we were playing an exhibition game in North Carolina, and I was talking with the general manager," he recalls. "A lady called and said, 'What time does the game start?' He said, 'What time can you get here?' That's kind of the way it was back then."

With the exception of Bailey Howell, Tormohlen had dominated most of the big men he faced in college. Upon entering the pro ranks, he quickly realized his dominating days were over. "After I got into the NBA, I discovered I was not as good as I thought," he says. "There were only eight teams in the league then, which meant I had to go head-to-head with Wilt [Chamberlain] and [Bill] Russell every week or so. That brought me down to Earth."

However Hall of Famers Chamberlain and Russell weren't the only NBA standouts to give Tormohlen trouble. "Nate Thurmond was really good, and so was Johnny Kerr," he recalls. "There were no easy games. Today you've got Shaq [Shaquille O'Neal] and [Tim] Duncan, then you might get an easy one or two. There were no easy ones back then. You couldn't go inside against Russell and Thurmond. You'd move outside and hope that J [jump shot] goes."

Still, the opponent he dreaded most was a relatively unknown player named Bob Ferry. Lacking the skills of Chamberlain and Russell, he offset his shortage of finesse with an abundance of aggressiveness. "If you went for a rebound, he'd be all over your back," Tormohlen recalls. "He'd say, 'I'm sorry, Gene,' but the next time a ball came off the backboard, he'd be all over your back again. That's the way those guys played back then."

More bull than ballerina himself, Tormohlen picked up the nickname "Bumper" during a stint in the American Basketball League. Shortly after he was traded to the Kansas City Steers by Cleveland Pipers owner George Steinbrenner (who later purchased Major League Baseball's New York Yankees), Tormohlen got the nickname from 6'6", 245-pound teammate Bill Bridges. "We tangled the first day of practice," Tormohlen says, "and he said afterward he was going to call me Bumper because I bumped him around so much."

After one year spent honing his skills in the ABL, Bumper earned a spot on the Hawks NBA roster. The league wasn't exactly a hot ticket in those days, and player salaries reflected as much. Compared to the multi-million dollar contracts of today's stars, pros of the 1950s settled for chump change. "Guys like Pettit made around $30,000, but most of us were in the $10,000 to $15,000 range," Tormohlen says. "Even at those salaries, guys gave you 95 percent every night; some of them gave 100 percent. You don't get that kind of effort today. But if you didn't give 100 percent in those days, they'd break your plate [put you on waivers]."

After nine years giving and collecting bruises under NBA backboards, Tormohlen traded his uniform for a suit and tie. He served as an assistant coach for several NBA franchises, twice filling in as interim head coach. Those were not pleasant experiences, however. Knowing the interim coach's reign was temporary, the players did not show him the same respect they would give a full-time head coach. "As an interim coach, you're trying to clean up someone else's mess by the end of the year," Tormohlen says. "If you're going to be a coach, you've got to have full authority. You can't go in there as a weak sister. The players have to know you're 'The Man.' If you go in there any other way, you're going to be defeated."

Eventually Tormohlen shifted from coaching into the scouting end of basketball. The transition was smooth and permanent. "I really enjoy scouting," he says. "The best job in the NBA is being a player. Scouting is the second-best job in the league. Coaching is way down the list, as far as I'm concerned."

Although he relished the hard-nosed brand of basketball that existed in his era, Tormohlen thinks the advent of the shot clock and the 3-point basket have made the game even better. He points to the attendance figures as validation. "In those days we were drawing 6,500, and today they're drawing 19,000," he says. "The 3-point shot has done wonders for basketball—college or pro. If you're 8 points down with a minute to go, you've still got a chance. That makes it exciting for the fans and everybody involved.

"The shot clock's important, too. Nobody wants to see Marcus Haynes putting on a dribbling exhibition unless you're watching the Harlem Globetrotters. Watching a guy dribble the clock away is too boring."

Nothing about Gene Tormohlen was ever boring. Now in his sixties, he continues to reign as "Chairman of the Boards" at Tennessee—his school records seemingly out of reach. Still, he never would've squeezed all of those rebounds if he hadn't first squeezed all of those udders back in Holland, Indiana.

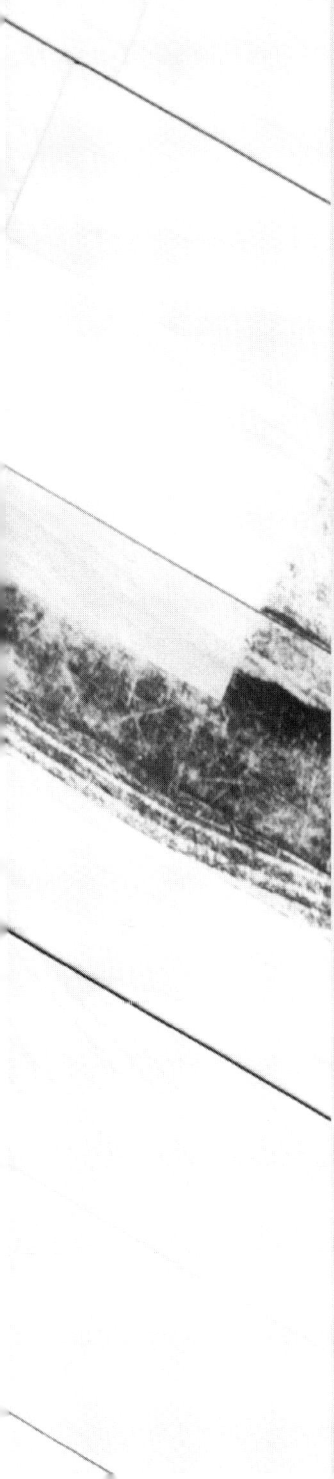

The Barnum of Basketball

In terms of pure entertainment value, pregame warm-ups for most college basketball programs of the 1960s and 1970s ranked somewhere between watching water boil and listening to a faucet drip. Then there was the Tennessee Volunteers.

Borrowing heavily from the Harlem Globetrotters, head coach Ray Mears concocted flashy dribbling and passing drills that his troops performed to the bouncy strains of "Sweet Georgia Brown." He figured the lighthearted approach would relax the players and amuse the onlookers.

However, the South Carolina Gamecocks were not amused as they watched the Volunteers warm up in Columbia on the night of December 6, 1969. Turning to teammate Tom Owens, Carolina guard Bobby Cremins grumbled, "Look at those fools. What the hell are they doing?"

The disdain was understandable. After all, the home-standing Gamecocks were ranked number one nationally and were fresh from a season-opening 88–66 romp at Auburn. The lightly regarded Volunteers—young, small, and untested—were 24-point underdogs. It was David versus Goliath with one notable difference: The Philistines had only one giant, while South Carolina featured three—Owens, Tom Riker, and John Ribock. "They had three guys bigger than anybody I could put on the floor," Mears recalled. "Ribock was 6'8" and built like a tank, and the other two were close to 7-footers."

The problem with David/Goliath matchups is they rarely produce the kind of dramatic ending that characterizes the biblical story. As a rule the towering giant crushes the undersized and outmanned opponent in short order. End of story.

But not always.

Like David, the Volunteers' only chance to prevail was to connect from long-range, utilizing the jump shot much as the fuzzy-cheeked shepherd utilized his slingshot. Unfortunately one of Tennessee's best outside shooters, Rudy Kinard, was recovering from knee surgery and was unable to play. That made the already imposing task a bit more daunting. Even Mears, who normally embraced the underdog role, figured this mountain might be too steep. "You know going in that your chances of beating the number-

Peltz: Ham of the Hardwood

Had he been born in medieval times, Roger Peltz probably would've been a court jester. Instead he settled for being a basketball court jester. A high school All-American in Royal Oaks, Michigan, he was an obscure reserve his first two seasons at Tennessee. That changed in 1969. He was still a reserve; he just wasn't obscure anymore.

After watching a troupe of unicyclists playing basketball, head coach Ray Mears suggested Peltz ride a unicycle to spice up pregame warmups. So while teammates were launching jump shots at the start of practice, Peltz was taking his first tentative steps on a borrowed unicycle.

When the 1969–70 season opened, Peltz rolled onto the playing floor atop his unicycle and stayed there while taking part in warmup drills. Encouraged by the rousing response, he decided to take his show on the road. Bad idea.

"When I came wheeling onto the court at Kentucky, they threw oranges at me," he says. "I didn't get hit but [teammate] Dicky Johnston did."

The 1970–71 season saw Peltz expand his repertoire, juggling three basketballs while riding his unicycle. When he debuted his new act, the roar of the crowd was deafening. Months after graduating, Peltz got another bizarre request from Mears: Wrestle a bear at halftime of the Volunteer Classic. A ham at heart, Peltz quickly agreed, although he conceded the idea was "kind of goofy."

Ultimately Peltz and Knoxville health spa operator John Paschal teamed up against a muzzled 450-pound bear. "It didn't have any teeth," Peltz says, "but it could gum you." The script called for the bear to deck one of the humans, then straddle him. When the other human climbed on the bear's back in an attempt to rescue his fallen partner, the bear would deliver the coup de grace.

"He'd put his paw behind your head and sort of flip you," Peltz recalls. "He didn't really flip you, but I timed it just right and it looked good. The crowd went wild."

Once a ham, always a ham.

one team on its home floor are a million-to-one shot," he said. "We just wanted to take it to them and try to make a game of it."

To the stunned disbelief of the partisan Carolina crowd, the Volunteers managed to do just that. Knowing the game could get ugly if the Gamecocks ever gained (a) a sizable lead and (b) the momentum, Mears instructed his players to be even more deliberate than usual. By passing the ball patiently until they created an open shot, the Volunteers hoped to keep the pace slow and the score low. They succeeded on both counts, trailing just 27–25 at halftime. "We didn't really believe we could win going in, but we began to believe it a few minutes into the game," Mears recalled. "From halftime on, there wasn't any question about it."

In addition to the three giants who comprised its front line, Carolina's starting unit featured a talented backcourt of Cremins and John Roche. Roche had been the Atlantic Coast Conference's Player of the Year as a sophomore the previous season; Cremins had a great mind for the game that eventually earned him the head coaching job at Georgia Tech.

Tennessee countered with 6'5" Don Johnson, 6'1" Jimmy England, 6'10" Bobby Croft, 6'6" Jim Woodall, and Kinard's replacement, 6'3" Kerry Myers. Since his starters couldn't match up with Carolina's imposing personnel, Mears knew his reserves would be totally overmatched . . . so he didn't play any. Tennessee's starting five gutted out the full forty minutes. "If you can train people to run a 26-mile marathon, you can train people to play a forty-minute basketball game," Mears explained. "Besides, it was a very slow-moving game."

That was because Carolina coach Frank McGuire inexplicably allowed Tennessee to dictate the tempo. The more time Mears's men exhausted dribbling and passing the ball, the less

Ray Mears's intensity nearly defied description.

time they had to spend trying to contain the talented Gamecocks. "They helped keep us in the game by playing a 2-3 zone," Mears said. "They weren't giving us any pressure, and that made it easy for us to do what we wanted."

Meanwhile Tennessee played a matchup zone defense that befuddled the Gamecocks. With England (20 points) and Johnson (18) connecting from outside, the Vols carried a 9-point lead into the game's final three minutes. What happened next, however, was the fulfillment of Mears's worst nightmare. Carolina went to a full-court press that rattled the visiting Volunteers and energized the home crowd.

Rallying furiously, the Gamecocks crept within a point as the game neared its end. Ultimately the outcome hinged on a 20-foot jump shot Roche unloaded a split-second before the buzzer. An eerie silence enveloped the arena as the ball floated toward the basket. When it bounced harmlessly off the rim, Tennessee's reserves finally left the bench—racing onto the court to celebrate a 55–54 victory that ranks as perhaps the greatest upset in program history. If that wasn't Ray Mears's finest hour as Tennessee's coach, it was awfully close. "It was one of the big ones," he conceded. "They [Gamecocks] had a great team and could've won the national title that year."

To commemorate the occasion, close friend Ken Rice presented Mears with a stuffed gamecock that ranks among the coach's prized possessions. Meanwhile, England presented his coach with the ultimate compliment. "We played pretty good," he said. "But you've got to credit that one to Coach Mears. He convinced us we could beat a team we had no business beating."

The fact is, Ramon Mears could convince just about anyone of just about anything. Even as a child he exhibited remarkable determination and perseverance. He grew up in tiny Dover, Ohio, a town known for producing two things—steel and basketball players. Three steel mills were a testament to the former; two state titles and a runner-up finish underscored the latter. "We had a lot of great basketball players there," Mears recalled. "I just wasn't one of them."

Still, his dedication to the game kept him playing until he was diagnosed with tuberculosis as a sophomore at Cadiz High School. Unable to quit the game cold turkey, he began coaching the Dover Avenue Elementary sixth-grade team. When his boys won the city championship, Mears realized he had a knack for molding individuals into a team concept. The course for his life was set.

With his illness in remission, Mears rejoined the Cadiz High School basketball team for his junior and senior seasons. Upon graduating, he worked six twelve-hour days per week in a steel mill until he had saved enough money to enroll at Miami of Ohio. He walked on with the basketball squad, where his teammates included Ara Parseghian, later to become head football coach at Notre Dame. Mears worked so hard that head coach Blue Foster offered him a scholarship prior to his senior season. Mears declined because "I wanted to say I worked my way through college."

After graduating he coached a few years at the high school level and then landed a job as headman at Wittenberg University in Springfield, Ohio. He guided the program to 121 victories in 144 games and three NCAA college-division national championship games—winning one. Then he left for Tennessee, which was coming off a 4–19 disaster in 1961–62.

Now thirty-five and facing his biggest challenge since tuberculosis, Mears considered himself "the best coach in the country," and he set out to prove it. "I wanted to play Adolph Rupp," he recalled, referring to the legendary Kentucky coach. "I always liked to play the best, and that's why I wanted the job at Tennessee."

Knowing he had inherited a program in decline, Mears worked even harder than usual to revive it. He worked so hard, in fact, that he began suffering dizzy spells shortly after taking the Vol reins. Diagnosed with exhaustion, he started taking what he called a "get-up-and-go pill." When these led to chronic insomnia, he began taking sleeping pills. Sadly they made his life worse instead of better. "The pill would last about a half-hour, then I'd wake up," he recalled. "I couldn't read and I couldn't watch television because I would see monsters coming out of the television."

Following a brief vacation Mears returned in time to guide his 1962–63 Volunteers to a 5–0 start. Then, following back-to-back road losses, he traveled to El Paso, Texas, for the Sun Bowl Classic tournament. His team was trounced 77–57 by Texas Western in the opening round, but the breakdowns that occurred on the floor were mild compared to the one that occurred on the Volunteer bench. Mears inexplicably strode to the opposite end of the floor and began examining the underside of the bleachers. When some players asked what he was looking for, the bewildered coach replied, "I don't know."

Realizing he was a sick man, he turned the team over to assistant coach Bill Gibbs and underwent shock treatments at a Virginia psychiatric hospital. Those treatments may have saved his life.

When Mears returned for the 1963–64 season, Tennessee basketball would never be the same. Just one year removed from a 4–19 debacle, the Volunteers went 16–8 overall and 9–5 in Southeastern Conference play. They even posted two upsets of in-state rival Vanderbilt, which was ranked in the national top ten that season.

The Volunteer program took another big step in 1964–65, thrashing Rupp's Kentucky Wildcats 77–58 en route to a 20–5 record that earned a number seventeen national ranking from United Press International. But the biggest step came in 1966–67, when the "Fearless Five" swept Kentucky, went 15–3 in league play, and captured Tennessee's first Southeastern Conference title in twenty-two years. That team finished the season ranked number eight nationally by the Associated Press.

Although Mears excelled in games, he was even better at gamesmanship. Shortly before facing Kentucky in Lexington one year, he read an article glorifying Rupp as "The Man in the Brown Suit." Mears immediately went shopping. "I didn't have anything but blue suits, but I went out and bought a $15 brown suit, then wore it to shake hands with him in the middle of the floor before the game," the Vol coach recalled. "I said, 'Rupp, I've got my brown suit on.'" Without comment Rupp turned and strode to the locker room. He remained there as his team completed its pregame warm-ups, boiling with rage.

Mears picked up the story at this point: "Kentucky's equipment manager told me later that Rupp went into the locker room, kicked the chairs all around, and said, 'That G— damned Mears knows I wear brown suits! What's he trying to do?'" What Mears was trying to do was unnerve his esteemed rival. Obviously he succeeded, but the talented Wildcats still won the game.

Mears used psychology on his players as well as his opponents, especially when it came to playing Kentucky. One time he hung a photo of Rupp on a basement door at Alumni Gym, then encouraged the Volunteers to throw darts at it on their way

The Pride of Sandy Hook

No fiction writer could script a more comical character than Orbie Lee Bowling of Sandy Hook, Kentucky. Knowing he was a joke waiting for a punchline, Orb made the first wisecrack shortly after arriving in Knoxville as a Volunteer freshman in the fall of 1959. "We live so far back in the sticks," he said, "that we don't get the [Saturday night] Grand Ole Opry until Monday night."

It was fortunate that Bowling could laugh at himself because everyone else did, too. Ordered by a music appreciation instructor to bring a classical recording to the next gathering, Orb showed up with a bluegrass tune by Lester Flatt and Earl Scruggs.

Bowling scored 31 points in a 1962 defeat of heavily favored Vanderbilt, yet his greatest achievement occurred the following year: He brought down the house during one of head coach Ray Mears's no-nonsense practices. Mears, who always paid meticulous attention to detail, spent several minutes explaining precisely what he wanted on the center jump—where the ball should be tipped in various situations, where each player was to position himself, et cetera. Finally satisfied that he had covered all the bases, Mears turned to Bowling and asked, "OK, you're jumping center. Now who are *you* going to tip it to?"

There was an awkward silence as the unsophisticated backwoods boy pondered his options. Finally Orb drawled his response: "Coach, if you were jumpin' center, who would you tip it to?"

Mears's face was expressionless for several seconds. When the headman burst into laughter, Orb's teammates immediately followed suit.

to and from the practice floor each day. "We beat Kentucky that week," Mears noted, "but [athletics director] Bob Woodruff wasn't happy. He had to buy a new door. Hell, I felt like it was worth a new door to beat Kentucky."

Rupp's reign as the Southeastern Conference's resident superstar was interrupted between 1967 and 1970. That's when a longhaired, floppy-socked, 6'5" string bean named Pete Maravich took the league—and all of college basketball—by storm. Son of Louisiana State head coach Press Maravich, Pete had the green light to shoot whenever the mood struck him . . . and it struck him often. A brilliant ball-handler with nifty moves and a mind-boggling knack for creating shots, "Pistol Pete" set NCAA scoring records that may never be broken.

Maravich was averaging more than 40 points per game as a Louisiana State sophomore when Tennessee got its first look at him. After scouting the Tigers' previous game, Vol aide Stu Aberdeen offered Tennessee's players these words of warning: "All I'm going to say about Pete Maravich is he might be the greatest basketball player who ever lived."

Most opponents conceded Maravich his 40 points and tried to contain Louisiana State's other players. But Mears, always spurred by a challenge, was determined to shut down the crowd-pleasing superstar. The Vol coach elected to play a box-and-one defense—four players covering specific zones, with quick-footed Billy Hann shadowing Pistol Pete all over the court. Hann was stunned to learn of the assignment. "It was a scary thing," he said. "When Coach Mears said to guard him, I was surprised. I wasn't really that good of a defensive player."

He didn't have to be. Whenever Maravich crossed midcourt, Hann would steer him toward side court, where another Vol would provide double-team help. If Maravich got within 20 feet of the basket, two Vols would help triple-team him.

Mears's plan worked in that first meeting . . . and the second . . . the third, fourth, fifth, and sixth. Although he averaged an all-time NCAA–record 44.2 points per game during his three-year college career, Maravich managed just 23 points per game against Tennessee, losing five of the six meetings.

"When you played Pete, you were actually afraid he would embarrass you," Hann recalled years later. "I don't ever remember feeling that way about another player. He was something special." Maravich was so special, in fact, that Vol guard Bill Justus said each visit Pistol Pete paid to Knoxville was "like the circus was in town."

Against Tennessee, however, Maravich proved to be a mere sideshow. His point production in six meetings ranged from a low of 17 to a high of 30. More often than not, The Pistol misfired against the Vols. "We were successful at that because we knew he was going to shoot about 80 percent of the time," Mears said. "We'd double-team and triple-team him. He took a lot of bad shots, but Pistol Pete kept on shooting."

Meanwhile the Volunteers kept on winning. They went 20–6 in 1967–68 and 21–7 in 1968–69. They slipped to 16–9 in 1969–70, but Mears still solidified his reputation as one of the sharpest minds in the game that season. Trailing Florida at Gainesville with mere seconds remaining, he was reluctant to order his players to foul, since this would give the Gators two free throws. Instead Mears asked for a time-out. Since he already had exhausted his supply of time-outs, he was charged with a technical foul . . . which was precisely what the Vol coach wanted.

"The rule at that time gave the opponent one free throw, then there was a jump ball," he recalled. "We had 6'10" Bobby

Billy Hann's career highlight may have been shutting down Pistol Pete Maravich.

Croft, so we figured we'd get the jump and get the ball back while only giving up one free throw. We actually used that more than once in the game." And each time the Vols used it, it worked. With Croft getting each jump ball, Tennessee swapped two points for one enough times to tie the score by the end of regulation. Although Florida prevailed in overtime, NCAA brass hastily revised the rule governing technical fouls to eliminate the loophole Mears had exploited.

The Volunteers returned to their winning ways in 1970–71 (21–7) and 1971–72 (19–6), sharing the Southeastern Conference title in the latter. Victories brought more and more fans to newly built Stokely Athletics Center, yet Mears wasn't happy unless all of the seats were filled. Determined to make Tennessee basketball a happening, he dubbed the Knoxville area "Big Orange Country"—the school colors being orange and white—and outfitted his team in gaudy orange blazers.

Of course the sight of Tennessee orange made students at opposing schools see red, particularly at in-state rival Vanderbilt. Booed lustily by the Vandy student section as he made his way to the dressing room prior to a game at Nashville one winter, Mears found the venom invigorating. He made a point of strolling past the student section on all subsequent trips to that gym, annoying his audience with each deliberate step. One year he sharpened the insult by enlisting 6'7" Vol javelin thrower Bill Skinner to wear one of the eye-catching orange blazers and serve as his personal bodyguard on the Vanderbilt trip. When an orange-and-white basketball Tennessee used for pregame warm-ups bounded into the student section, Mears dispatched the towering Skinner to retrieve it. "Without a word Bill heads into the student section and walks right up to the kid who had the ball," Mears recalled.

"The kid was so scared he threw the ball right to Skinner. We just about had a riot!"

Commodore coach Roy Skinner—no relation to Bill—blasted Mears for purposely inciting the Vanderbilt students. But the Vol coach figured his 7–2 record against Skinner on Vandy's home floor was all the justification that was needed. "I really don't care to go down in the record books as an SOB," Mears once said, "but neither am I going to change my habits just because some people don't approve."

For a promotional genius like Mears, gaudy jackets and "Big Orange Country" were only the beginning. In the late 1960s he convinced little-used Vol reserve Roger Peltz to spice up pregame festivities by juggling three basketballs while pedaling around on a unicycle. It was about this time that the colorful headman earned the nickname "The Barnum of Basketball." Ray Mears's reputation for showmanship had eclipsed his reputation for gamesmanship—no small feat.

He continued winning games and fans into the 1970s. He went 15–15 against mighty Kentucky, a program that had won twenty-five of twenty-six meetings prior to Mears's arrival. And he won three Southeastern Conference championships, spacing them at five-year intervals (1967, 1972, 1977). Still, the ultimate testament to the man is that he elevated a near-comatose Tennessee basketball program to such a level of popularity that the school eventually built 24,500-seat Thompson-Boling Arena. "I think my destiny was to be at Tennessee," he said.

Mears resigned in 1978 following fifteen unforgettable seasons now viewed as the Golden Age of Tennessee basketball. His legacy can be summed up in the numbers he left behind: 278 wins, 112 losses, a million memories.

One Versatile Volunteer

No one in his right mind would trade a Mercedes Benz for a Ford Edsel. But that's essentially what George Ronald "Ron" Widby had in mind when he visited the University of Tennessee basketball office in the spring of 1963. Widby, a senior at Knoxville's Fulton High School, wanted to trade his Vol football scholarship for a Vol basketball scholarship—the athletic equivalent of a Mercedes/Edsel swap.

Head basketball coach Ray Mears and assistant Bill Gibbs listened intently while the young man made his pitch. The problem was, they admired his spunk a lot more than his basketball skills. As a result their challenge was simple: How do we tell him "Thanks, but no thanks," tactfully enough to avoid insulting him? After an awkward silence, the two coaches finally responded. "They said they didn't know if I was the caliber of player to play in the Southeastern Conference," Widby recalls.

Most youngsters would have accepted the unflattering comment with a shrug, stared at the floor to hide their disappointment, and then made a hasty exit from the office. Widby made a hasty exit, all right, but first he said something the Volunteer coaches never expected: "If you don't have a basketball scholarship for me, I'll look elsewhere."

And he did. Widby visited Carson-Newman College in nearby Jefferson City. He also toured a couple of other campuses. However, the search for a new school left him feeling empty. "My heart wasn't in it," he says. "I really wanted to attend Tennessee." That represented quite a turnabout for Widby, who two years earlier hadn't given Volunteer basketball a second thought. The 1961–62 team was horrendous, limping home with a 4–19 record that cost head coach John Sines his job.

Widby's interest would blossom during his senior season at Fulton. Mears, a marketing genius, had brought a new level of excitement to Tennessee basketball by incorporating a generous helping of pregame pageantry. The new look included a bouncy pep band, marching majorettes, and flashy warm-up routines. The theatrics didn't end at tip-off, either. Mears put on quite a show during the games with his fiery courtside demeanor and penchant for gamesmanship. "Honestly the first time I saw pregame warm-ups I was a little shocked; it looked like a Harlem Globetrotters deal," Widby recalls. "It got the fans fired up, though. You could see within a month or so that Coach Mears had turned the program around."

Yet in the spring of 1963 it appeared Widby would never be a part of that program. He was still mulling the possibility of reneging on his Tennessee football scholarship when Mears met with head football coach Jim McDonald to discuss the basketball-or-else ultimatum. Impressed as much by the young man's nerve as his athleticism, the two coaches decided he could play basketball while remaining on a football scholarship.

That decision looked pretty smart four years later, when Ron Widby became the first athlete in school history to earn All-America recognition in both sports. It was an unprecedented ride, but it was one that began with an unfortunate fall. Widby broke his arm in the final game of his Fulton High football career. In retrospect that may have been the best break in Volunteer basketball history. After missing the first eight games of the Falcons hoops season—all losses—he suited up for game nine and promptly led the team to its first victory of 1962–63. He played so well thereafter that he earned all-state honors, despite missing roughly one-third of the season. "I had a good year in basketball," he recalls. "I felt it was my best sport, and I wanted to play basketball at Tennessee."

Once he convinced himself of this, Widby had to convince Mears and Gibbs. They in turn had to convince McDonald. After all of the convincing was complete, the pride of Fulton High School figured his gridiron days were over. He could not have been more mistaken.

When the Vol football team gathered for preseason drills that August, McDonald discovered that he needed to groom a punter for the future. Remembering how well Widby had punted in high school, the football coach paid a visit to Mears's office. Basically, he asked to borrow Widby during the fall. Mears—perhaps entertaining lingering doubts about the youngster's hoop skills—quickly pledged his support for the idea. "Coach Mears encouraged me," Widby recalls. "I'd done some punting in high school, so I figured that would be a pretty good job."

Combining football and basketball is normally quite a challenge. However, because his football duties consisted of merely punting the ball, Widby found the task relatively easy. "Each day I'd attend special-teams practice in football, then go over to Armory Fieldhouse, change clothes, and practice basketball," he says. "I'd played several sports in high school, so it seemed like no big deal."

The double duty may have been no big deal, but Ron Widby was a very big deal. Although freshmen were ineligible for varsity competition in 1963–64, his booming punts in football practice and his sensational scoring in freshman basketball games had fans of both sports eagerly awaiting his sophomore season. Spurred by the success of the frosh hoops squad, Widby was excited, too. "We had an awfully good freshman team—Mac Petty, Wes Coffman, Tom Hendrix, Tom Boerwinkle, Joe Pangrazio, and myself," he recalls. "We played around twenty-five games and only lost two. One of the losses was to a Kentucky team that had [future All-Americans] Pat Riley and Louis Dampier . . . and we beat them at our place."

As talented as those 1963–64 Volunteer freshmen were, however, all of them redshirted to get additional seasoning in 1964–65 except for one . . . Widby. Fewer than two years after hearing he might not be good enough to play in the Southeastern Conference, the 6'4" Knoxville native won a starting job and ranked among Tennessee's leading scorers. Even playing in a deliberate offense, Widby averaged an impressive 14.5 points per game as a sophomore in helping the Vols post an outstanding 20–5 record.

But individual exploits were never his aim. That's why he recalls the highlights of the 1964–65 season as "beating Kentucky in Knoxville and playing with A. W. Davis, one of the legends of Tennessee basketball." Of course Widby's respect for the legendary Davis didn't deter him from supplanting "The Rutledge Rifle" as the program's career scoring leader two years later.

After playing football all fall and basketball all winter, Widby figured he needed a way to pass the time in the spring. Trying out for the Vol baseball team, he won the starting job at first base and promptly batted .300. He finished his sophomore year with three varsity letters, having achieved first-team status in all three sports.

Widby was an even busier man as a junior, with an itinerary that peaked on December 17–18, 1965. After helping the basketball Vols beat Louisiana Tech 71–55 in round one of the Gulf South Classic at Shreveport, he boarded a private plane and flew to Houston, where he would represent the football Vols in the Bluebonnet Bowl at noon the following day.

Arriving in Houston around midnight, Widby was starving but had to settle for the only food on the team hotel's late-night menu—a sandwich. He somehow got enough nourishment and sleep to go out the next day and average 41 yards per punt in helping the football Vols beat Tulsa 27–6. Minutes later he jetted back to Shreveport for the Gulf South Classic finals. His timing was a little better. "I got there just in time for the pregame meal," he says.

Widby then concluded the most hectic twenty-six hours of his life by scoring 18 points to earn tournament most valuable

Ron Widby made threats in order to get a spot on Tennessee's basketball team, then made All-America.

player honors and lead the basketball Vols past Centenary 49–43 in the title game.

That wild weekend stood as the highlight of his 1965–66 season for twenty-five games. With an unimposing 17–8 record and one game left on the schedule, Widby & Company hoped to go out with a bang. That would not be easy considering the opponent. A top-ranked Kentucky team known as "Rupp's Runts" rolled into Knoxville with a 24–0 record and a condescending attitude. "When Kentucky came onto the court, they looked at us the way Tennessee looks at Vanderbilt in football," Widby recalls. "Adolph Rupp was a legend, and you just didn't beat him back then."

But Tennessee did. Widby made the final game at Armory Fieldhouse a memorable one, scoring a team high of 22 points in a stunning 69–62 upset. The ensuing celebration spilled off the court and onto campus streets and continued into the wee hours of the morning. "Beating Kentucky," Widby says, "was like climbing a mountain you didn't think you could climb." He finished the season with a 17.3 scoring average, nearly three points per game better than his sophomore year. Still, the best was yet to come.

After playing the football/basketball/baseball trifecta as a freshman and sophomore, Widby felt he needed a rest in the spring of 1966. "I was a little tired of one right after the other," he says. "I went to [baseball coach] Bill Wright following my sophomore year and said I wasn't going to play anymore." But when he came face to face with inactivity the following spring, Widby grew restless. "I was bored, so I went to [golf coach] Lloyd Foree and asked if I could play for the golf team." Gifted athlete that he was, Widby not only made the team but averaged in the mid-70s and emerged as one of the Vols' top golfers. "Golf was a lot easier than playing baseball had been," he says.

As a result Widby was more rested than usual when he reported for the start of basketball practice in 1966–67. With four of the top six players gone from the previous year's team, Tennessee faced a rebuilding job. Widby, the team's only senior, was the obvious choice for captain. Two redshirt juniors—Boerwinkle and Hendrix—along with a pair of sophomore guards—Billy Hann and Bill Justus—joined him in the starting unit.

Boerwinkle, a 7-footer, had been so raw coming out of a Lexington, Kentucky, prep school three years earlier that the hometown Wildcats didn't give him a second look. Although he acknowledged that the big guy "had a hard time walking and chewing gum at the same time," Mears rolled the dice and signed him, hoping he eventually could develop him into a decent player. Oddly enough, the grooming process turned out to be a *brooming* process.

Since none of the other Vols was tall enough to challenge Boerwinkle's shots in practice, 5'5" assistant coach Stu Aberdeen assumed the task. Utilizing a straw broom to offset the severe height disadvantage, Aberdeen would swing it in front of Boerwinkle's face on shot attempts, often smacking the big man in the head, forearms, and shoulders. Normally good-natured, Boerwinkle took so many shots from the broom that he eventually turned on his tormentor. "One time Tom got tired of that broom hitting him and chased Coach Aberdeen right out of the gym," Widby recalls with a laugh.

Boerwinkle wasn't the only Vol to be swept away in practice, however. "I went against the broom also," Widby says. "It made you a little tougher, but I'll tell you this: Coach Aberdeen could really tick you off with that thing."

Given the doubts about Boerwinkle's agility and the rest of the cast's ability, most preseason analysts pegged the Vols for fifth or sixth

Seven-footer Tom Boerwinkle went from awkward to awesome during his Tennessee career.

How's That for Scoring Punch?

High-scoring Ron Widby made a lot of shots during his college career, but one shot got him a reprimand from a Vol assistant. It was a shot to the jaw of a Tennessee teammate.

In preparation for a 1967 road trip to face Auburn and Alabama, two very physical teams, Tennessee's coaches decided to toughen up their starters a bit. Toward this end, they instructed the scout squad to use roughhouse tactics in practice. Happy to oblige, the scout teamers threw themselves into the task with remarkable zeal. They enthusiastically grabbed, shoved, elbowed, and kneed the first teamers throughout that day's workout. Through it all, head coach Ray Mears never blew his whistle. No blood, no foul.

"It was tougher than a lot of football practices," recalled Widby, who played both sports. "I got smacked in the face, and both arms were bruised." Deciding he'd had enough, Widby warned freshman Mike Humphries to tone down the rough stuff. The words fell on deaf ears. "He hit me again on the very next play," Widby noted. "I turned around and decked him with one punch."

Clearly flustered by the violent reaction, assistant coach Stu Aberdeen rushed to Widby's side. Knowing he was about to be chastised, the player braced himself for a lecture on team unity. Instead he got a scolding that almost put him on the floor next to Humphries. "Ronnie, Ronnie, you mustn't do that," Aberdeen chirped in his high-pitched, nasal voice. "What if you broke your hand?"

place in the rugged Southeastern Conference race. Mears knew the talent around Widby was largely unproven, so he instructed his senior standout to shoulder most of the scoring burden.

With Widby producing the bulk of the points, Tennessee won its first four games of 1966–67. When the Volunteers suffered back-to-back losses to Bradley (60–53) and Boston College (68–61) at the Sugar Bowl Classic in New Orleans, however, some analysts labeled Tennessee a "one-man team" doomed to failure. Widby felt the characterization insulted his teammates and wasn't timid about saying so. "They can play," he said. "This is the best Tennessee team I've played on, and it's no one-man team, either. Wait and see."

The fact that Widby scored roughly half of Tennessee's points in many games was more a reflection of the Volunteer system than the lack of scoring punch from his teammates. "In Coach Mears' system everybody has a job to do," he said. "My primary job was to shoot and score. That was what I was directed to do; that's how we were successful. Everybody had a certain role, and if everybody played his role, we'd get positive results."

Those positive results would soon be evident. The lost weekend at New Orleans seemed to galvanize the Volunteers and change the course of their season. "Those two losses probably turned our season around," Widby recalls. "They sure left an awful taste in your mouth."

Whatever spurred them, the Vols won nine of their next ten games. Included in this stretch was an unforgettable 52–50 double-overtime upset of Kentucky in Lexington. Undercut on a driving layup one game earlier, Widby took a nasty spill that left him with a severely sprained right wrist. As a result he scored a season low of 8 points against the Big Blue, despite playing all fifty minutes. "My wrist hurt so bad I thought it was broken," Widby says. "I couldn't even hit the rim from the free-throw line, but everybody else stepped up big-time. The other guys always had the capability to score, but they were content to play other roles."

Tennessee's players knew Widby was hurting, but Kentucky's players didn't. Thus the Vol captain played the role of decoy for much of the evening. "I was there more for moral support and rebounds," he says. "My teammates knew I was hurting and they came to the forefront with their game. We took out an awfully good basketball team on their home floor without our leading scorer. That was one of the highlights of that season."

Another highlight occurred a few weeks later in Widby's final home appearance as a Volunteer. Tennessee needed to beat visiting Louisiana State to clinch at least a tie for the Southeastern Conference championship, so the stakes were high. The Vols built a comfortable lead in the second half, but then something downright bizarre happened. Widby passed to Justus, who immediately threw the ball back to him. Widby then passed to Hann, who also returned the ball to the captain. Widby shot and scored. On the next Tennessee possession, Widby passed to Hendrix, who immediately returned the feed. Widby shot and scored. The more Widby tried to get rid of the ball, the more it wound up in his hands. "Every time I'd pass the ball to somebody, they'd pass it right back," he recalls. "Nobody would shoot." Finally, the homegrown senior realized what his teammates were doing. "After a while I figured out what was going on," he says. "They wanted me to get the Fieldhouse scoring record."

The record, 47 points, had been set eleven years earlier by Carl Widseth. With the hot-shooting Widby taking almost every Tennessee shot down the stretch, he eventually eclipsed it. Once

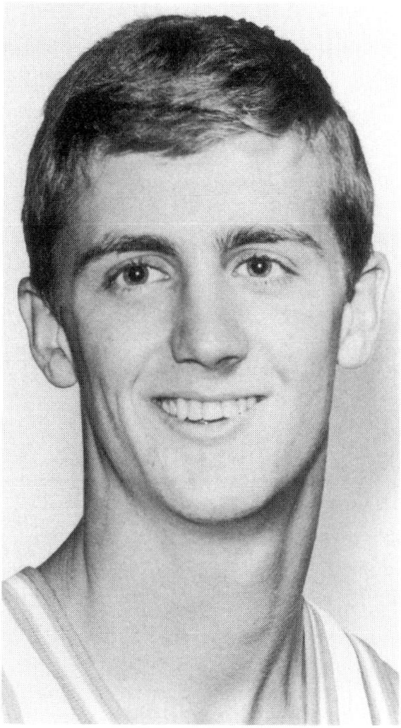

Sophomore Bill Justus was a key member of the "Fearless Five."

he posted his fiftieth point, he got the rest of the night off. "Right after I scored the basket that broke the record, Coach Mears took me out of the game," Widby recalls. "I got a standing ovation from the crowd and from my teammates. That was really inspiring. That put tears in my eyes and a knot in my throat; it still does to this day. For a kid raised in Knoxville who wanted to play for Tennessee all of his life, that was quite a feeling."

Widby, who hit 19 of 39 field-goal tries and 12 of 14 free-throw tries during the record-breaking performance, was applauded by both the winning and losing coaches following the game. "Our players paid the greatest tribute you can give another

Tom Hendrix's late basket helped the Vols win the 1967 SEC title.

player," Mears said. "I never said one thing about Ron Widby setting records. I wanted to win the game and get the tie for the title. It was their [teammates'] idea to give Ron the ball."

Louisiana State's Press Maravich was even more complimentary in saluting Widby's 50-point outing. "Ron Widby is a great player," the Tiger coach said. "I thought he'd get 100."

As rewarding as scoring 50 points in his final home game had been, Widby knew the potential for an even bigger thrill loomed mere days in the future. A victory at Mississippi State in the regular-season finale would give the Volunteers the conference title outright. Conversely a loss would force a three-way playoff between Tennessee, Florida, and Vanderbilt to determine the league's representative to the NCAA Tournament. The game was set for the night of March 6, 1967, and it would be a long night for the Vols. Literally.

Widby scored in the final minute to put Tennessee on top, but Mississippi State got a basket with seven seconds left in regulation to tie the score at 64–64. The first overtime ended 66–66. Widby hit 3 field goals in the second extra period, but Justus missed 2 free throws with four seconds left, and the score was knotted at 72–all. The home-standing Bulldogs produced the first 4 points of the third overtime, but Widby and Hendrix scored a bucket each to tie the score. Justus, fouled again with four seconds left, atoned for his earlier misses by hitting both tries. When Mississippi State's desperation shot missed at the buzzer, Tennessee had a 78–76 victory, its first conference title in twenty-four years and its first NCAA Tournament bid ever.

"That night was the highlight of my college career," says Widby, who played all fifty-five minutes of the marathon affair. "Three overtimes was taxing, but you didn't think about it at the time, and you didn't really feel tired. I think we played that game with six players. Wes Coffman came in for Hendrix when he got in some early foul trouble, and he came in for Boerwinkle whenever Tom got tired. But I played the entire game; so did Hann and Justus."

Following the long game, Tennessee's players took long celebratory showers. A Knoxville sportswriter joined the waterlogged fun, albeit unwillingly. "I told Marvin West [of the *Knoxville News-Sentinel*] before the season that we were going to win the SEC that year," Widby says. "He kind of laughed. When we did win it, I looked him up and threw him in the shower."

Watch Your Step, Coach

Even his staunchest critics must admit Ray Mears had one of the most creative minds in the history of college basketball. He had an uncanny knack for outsmarting foes . . . and officials. The most dramatic example of the latter occurred in a game at Ole Miss in the late 1960s. Enraged by a call that went against his Vols, Mears stormed onto the playing floor to confront referee John McPherson. This was an automatic technical foul, but McPherson decided to make the punishment even more severe than usual. Nodding toward the Tennessee sidelines, McPherson snapped, "It's going to cost you one technical foul for each step it takes you to get back to the bench."

Mears's feet were still but his brain was going a hundred miles per hour. With a smug grin, he beckoned assistant coaches Stu Aberdeen and Sid Hatfield to pick him up and carry him back to the bench. Only a middleweight in those days, Mears never let his feet touch the ground on the return trip to the sidelines. Clearly outmaneuvered, McPherson knew he was a beaten man. "OK, you got me that time," he grumbled. "But if you ever come out here again, I'll get you."

There was considerable irony attached to the momentous victory in Starkville. At the conclusion of Tennessee's first preseason practice, Aberdeen put the players through a wicked conditioning workout. After thirty minutes of agonizing wind sprints, the Volunteers were totally spent. Boerwinkle turned to Widby and, literally wheezing, said: "Ron, you're the captain. We can't do this every day." Looking back, Widby says: "I think Boerwinkle would've chased Aberdeen out of the gym again that day, except he couldn't move."

The captain passed along Boerwinkle's concern to Mears following the taxing workout, and the headman promised Aberdeen would tone down the conditioning drills a bit thereafter. "It's odd when you think back on it," Widby says. "Coach Aberdeen spent all of that time building our stamina, then we end up playing a three-overtime game to end the season."

That game would've provided a fitting end to a Cinderella season, but the Volunteers had one more mountain to climb. They still had a date with All-American Don May and the Dayton Flyers in round one of the sixteen-team NCAA Tournament. Perhaps drained by the emotional win at Starkville, Tennessee's players never quite found their rhythm. Still, they trailed by only 1 point entering the final minute. Mears put the game in Widby's hands by ordering the Vols to run a play that gave their senior captain the final shot.

The plan was sound, but the shot rimmed out, leaving Tennessee on the short end of a 53–52 score. Widby's glorious career had ended on a somewhat sour note. "It wasn't difficult to lose, but it was difficult to see that shot not go down," he says. "You feel like it's on your shoulders, and it took me a while to get over that. But I had great teammates. Nobody ever said, 'You're the big scorer. You're supposed to make it.'"

Certainly, blaming the captain for the NCAA loss would've been insane. For one thing, he carried the team for most of the season, averaging a school-record 22.1 points per game. For another, he wasn't the only Vol who struggled against Dayton. "I don't think we were nervous or awed by being in the NCAA," Widby says. "We were confident we could beat 'em, but we fell one point short. We played a decent game, but I didn't play up to my potential."

That loss grew even more painful when Dayton advanced to the NCAA title game, where the Flyers fell to UCLA. "It really sticks in your craw because you wonder if you might have done what they did," Widby says. "Who knows? If we'd gotten by that first game, maybe we could've gone to the finals."

If Widby entertained any regrets, they were misplaced. He compiled perhaps the greatest season any Volunteer athlete ever had during the 1966–67 school year. On the gridiron he led the NCAA in punting with a 43.8-yard average. On the hardwood he led the Southeastern Conference in scoring with a 22.1 average. In the process he became the first Tennessee athlete ever to earn All-America recognition in both sports.

Even after Widby's college days ended, his days as a football/basketball player continued. He spent the 1967–68 National Football, League season with the Dallas Cowboys and then served as sixth man for the New Orleans Buccaneers of the American Basketball Association. When the fall of 1968 rolled around, he decided to return to the Cowboys and focus exclusively on football. "I couldn't do 'em both because the ABA season was just too much travel," he says. "I told my wife if I made it in football, I'd give up basketball. In football you're only gone on Saturday night. In basketball you're playing eighty-some games."

On November 3, 1968—two days before the birth of his first child—Widby boomed an 84-yard punt for Dallas that still stands as the franchise record. He earned a Super Bowl ring with the Cowboys in 1971 and made the Pro Bowl that same season.

After four years with Dallas and two with the Green Bay Packers, Widby retired from football . . . but not from sports. Upon turning fifty he tried to qualify for the Professional Golf Association Seniors Tour. He reached the finals but missed earning a tour card and decided not to try again.

Considering all of the memories he made while playing all of those sports, Widby's difficulty singling out one thrill that stands above the rest is understandable. "Winning a Super Bowl is something everybody dreams of," he says. "And going to the Pro Bowl that same year meant a lot to me. Still, I'm not sure if any of that overshadows my senior year at Tennessee. Winning the league title in my hometown was special."

The fact he scored 50 points in the game was just gravy. Interestingly enough, that record stood for twenty years. Tony White broke it with 51 points against Auburn on February 14, 1987. "Frankly, I didn't think it would stand for twenty years," Widby says. Then, with a chuckle, he added, "Of course, if we'd had the three-pointer back then, I might still have the record."

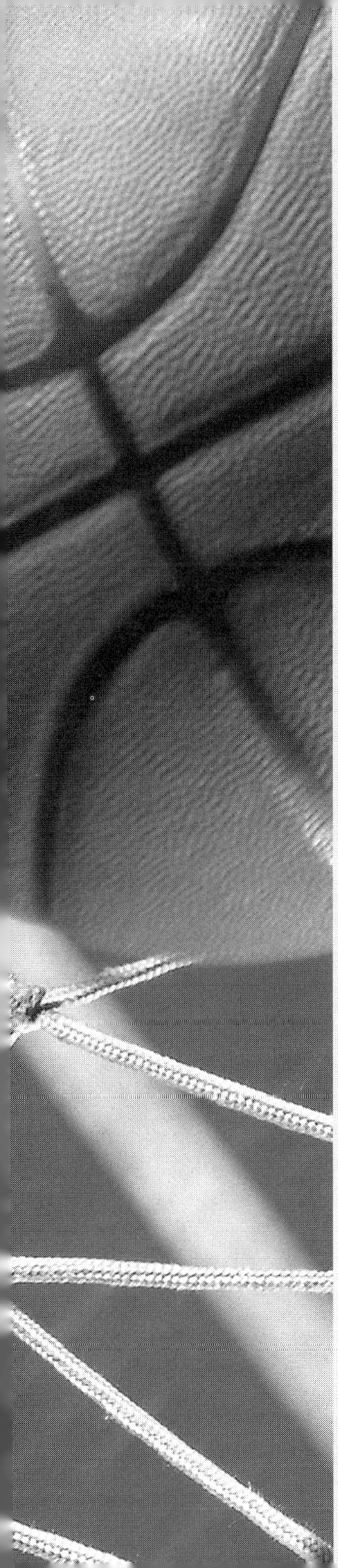

The Ernie and Bernie Show

Sometimes when the sporting gods are feeling mischievous, they place two stars on the same orbit Ruth and Gehrig, Davis and Blanchard, Koufax and Drysdale, Unitas and Berry . . . Ernie and Bernie. For stars of such magnitude, full names are unnecessary. During their Tennessee basketball days, Ernie Grunfeld and Bernard King were known simply as "Ernie and Bernie" to friend and foe alike . . . and they had plenty of each. The affable Grunfeld probably had a few more friends. The volatile King probably had a few more enemies, particularly in the Bluegrass State.

Following an 88–82 loss to Kentucky on January 13, 1975 at Lexington's Rupp Arena, King was showered with debris and verbal abuse as he left the playing floor. The Volunteer freshman had developed a pretty hard shell growing up in a New York City ghetto, but this unprovoked attack got under his skin. Moments later, dissecting the game for the assembled media, he issued a warning to the Cats, their fans, their program, and everything Blue. "They will *never* beat us again as long as I play at Tennessee," King vowed. And they never did.

King and Grunfeld avenged the Lexington loss later that season in Knoxville and then helped the Big Orange sweep the Big Blue in 1975–76 and 1976–77. Nearly three decades later, the Ernie and Bernie years still rank as the most successful and exciting in Volunteer basketball history.

So why did Grunfeld and King leave the Big Apple to become the primary ingredients in a Big Orange stew? The answer was a Big Orange Stu . . . as in Stu Aberdeen. Tennessee's diminutive assistant coach was a recruiting giant, despite his 5'5" frame. When he went to New York in the spring of 1973 to scout Grunfeld, the course of Volunteer basketball was forever changed.

Aberdeen and wife, Lynn, were moving into a new home, yet he spent fifty days of a two-month stretch in New York on his mission. "The City That Never Sleeps" was an appropriate place for a Vol aide who wasn't getting a whole lot of shut-eye himself. "I remember one time when I flew back from New York, got home about 7:00 P.M., worked all night packing up the house for the moving people, and then left out again for New York at 8:00

Diminutive Stu Aberdeen played a huge role in casting the Ernie and Bernie Show.

the next morning without getting a wink of sleep," Aberdeen recalled.

The Vol aide's persistence was unmatched and almost unimaginable. One day as he strolled into the lobby of his Manhattan hotel, Aberdeen noted a recruiter from a rival school leaving, suitcase in hand. "OK, you crazy son of a bitch; you stay if you want to," the rival recruiter said. "I'm leaving."

Aberdeen stayed and swayed his quarry. Grunfeld eventually relented and signed on the dotted line about the same time Tennessee offered a scholarship to close friend Jerry Finestone. Aberdeen slept much better thereafter. For the four years that followed, opposing coaches slept a whole lot worse.

Grunfeld, a 6'5" small forward who picked the Volunteers over Michigan and Syracuse, summed up his choice in one sentence: "I liked Coach Aberdeen, and I thought I had a chance to play as a freshman." He played, all right. The rookie known as "Ernie G" started every game and averaged 17.4 points per outing to earn first-team All-Southeastern Conference and first-team Freshman All-America recognition.

Given the overwhelming contribution Tennessee got from Grunfeld in 1973–74, Aberdeen felt compelled to return to New York's playgrounds that summer in pursuit of King, a 6'7" post player with a combative disposition and lightning quick moves. Aberdeen figured he was in for another long, drawn-out recruiting battle. "When it came time to go after Bernard King, I was expecting another two-month stand," the Vol aide recalled. "I had two big suitcases full of clothes packed. When I left, Lynn said, 'See you next year.'"

Whereas Stu and Lynn were a marriage made in compromise, Ernie and Bernie would prove to be a marriage made in basketball heaven. The addition of King made Grunfeld an even better player . . . but not right away. Six days before the 1974–75 season was to begin, Grunfeld broke his right wrist during a preseason scrimmage against Western Kentucky. The Ernie and Bernie Show would have to wait. In the meantime there was the Bernie Show.

With Grunfeld sidelined, King made his collegiate debut a memorable one, scoring 42 points as Tennessee beat Wisconsin-Milwaukee in the opener. By the time Ernie rejoined the team three weeks into the season, the Volunteers boasted a 5–1 record, a souped-up attack, and an unprecedented level of popularity. When Grunfeld and King finally teamed up in game seven, the result was a 115–66 annihilation of Vermont. "On the court Ernie's dynamic," Volunteer point guard Rodney Woods noted. "The night he came back after being hurt, the place just went wild. Some players' personalities are reflected in the way a crowd reacts to them, and he's one of those players."

That Grunfeld wound up at Tennessee was no small miracle. Born of Jewish parents in Romania, he and his family left to escape religious persecution when Ernie was nine years old. Young Grunfeld was saddened when friends wept during his departure, but he was all smiles when the plane landed in New York City. Years later he could still recite the arrival time— "April 13, 1964, 11:30 A.M. on a Pan-Am jet."

The Grunfelds settled in Forest Hills, a New York City suburb, and set about looking for ways to blend into their new surroundings. Ernie soon found his way onto the playgrounds. He was ten years old the first time he touched a basketball, but he quickly made up for lost time. "I wanted to belong in a new neighborhood," he said, "and I found out fast if you wanted to belong you'd better play basketball."

22
REBELS
20

By the ninth grade Ernie was honing his hoops skills between five and six hours every day—two hours with his junior high school team and the rest on the playgrounds. The crash course paid dividends. He averaged 18 points per game as a sophomore at Forest Hills High and then improved to 20.9 points and 18.8 rebounds per game as a junior, earning second-team All-City honors. His numbers dropped a bit as a senior—16.5 points and 17 rebounds per game—but he was tabbed first-team All-City and high school All-America. Roughly 200 colleges recruited him, but Aberdeen won out with persistence and an appeal to Ernie's ethnic pride. On Grunfeld's official visit to Tennessee, the Vol aide took him to visit many of Knoxville's more successful Jewish businessmen.

If signing a Jewish kid from Romania represented an unlikely first step in head coach Ray Mears's quest to build a national powerhouse at Tennessee, step two would prove just as unimaginable—landing an inner-city black kid from Brooklyn. It seemed an impossible dream, but the strength of Aberdeen's will—and his marriage—carried the day once more.

Days after King made an official visit to Tennessee, Aberdeen traveled to Brooklyn for a follow-up meeting. A preliminary chat with King's prep coach, Ken Kern, did not bode well. "Don't try to sign Bernard on this trip," Kern said. "He has some other schools to visit and just isn't ready yet." After agreeing to withhold his sales pitch, Aberdeen paid a visit to King's home. The conversation was predictable; the conclusion was not. "We had our visit, and I was getting ready to leave," Aberdeen recalled. "I just made the usual little talk about our being completely sold on him and

Ernie Grunfeld combined a soft shooting touch and a rugged style of play.

about how much we wanted him at Tennessee, when all of a sudden he told me he was ready to sign, right then and there. It floored me."

Remembering his earlier promise to Kern, Aberdeen found himself in an unexpected bind. He waited anxiously as King telephoned his high school coach to convey his decision. Sure enough Kern asked to speak with Aberdeen. "I had to get on the phone to assure Ken that I hadn't broken my word and done any high-pressure job," the Volunteer assistant recalled.

In truth, the only "high-pressure job" was the one facing Tennessee's head basketball coach. Knowing he now had the makings of a great team, the high-strung Mears grew even more intense. The pursuit of excellence gave way to the pursuit of a national title.

Long known for his deliberate style of play, Mears decided to pick up the pace now that he had two of basketball's brightest young stars. He installed a fast-break offense designed to get transition layups for King and transition jump shots for Grunfeld. By February the high-octane Volunteers sported a 13–3 record, a number eighteen national ranking, and a growing legion of detractors. One of them contacted the NCAA and suggested that King's high school transcript had been doctored.

King missed the next three games—one while an NCAA investigation cleared him of the transcript allegations, two more due to injury—and Tennessee promptly lost all three. King finally returned to action on February 13, just in time for a put-up-or-shut-up rematch with Kentucky. The fourth-ranked Wildcats hadn't forgotten the angry vow the brash freshman had made one month earlier. Apparently Bernard hadn't forgotten either. He helped guide the Volunteers to a 103–98 victory.

Tennessee finished the season 18–8 and clearly on the upswing. King, though only a freshman, led the Southeastern Conference in scoring (26.4 points per game) and led the NCAA in field-goal percentage (62.2). Tabbed the league's player of the year, he was joined on the first-team all-conference squad by Grunfeld, who averaged 23.8 points per game. The future had never looked brighter.

After improving his quickness and shooting range during the off-season, Grunfeld blossomed as a junior in 1975–76. He was virtually unstoppable during one four-game stretch that began with back-to-back 36-point efforts against Pennsylvania and Tulane. He followed with 25 points and 14 rebounds in the Southeastern Conference opener against Georgia and then scored a career-high 43 points against Kentucky.

During the four-game outburst, Ernie G. averaged 35 points per game while shooting 57.3 percent from the field and 88.4 percent from the foul line. All of this left his head coach grasping for suitable superlatives. "There are some things on a basketball court that Ernie does better than any forward I have ever seen," Mears said. "He can whirl out of a pressure situation better than anybody. He can power his way to the boards. And he is as good at one-on-one basketball as I have seen."

One month later, with the Vols 16–2 and ranked number eight nationally, Grunfeld and King graced the cover of *Sports Illustrated* magazine under the heading "Double Trouble from Tennessee." The Ernie and Bernie Show had become an off-Broadway hit, but the significance was lost on the dynamic duo. "At the time it happened, it was no big deal to us," Grunfeld recalled years later. "It was like, 'Great, we're on the cover. When's the next game?' "

Grunfeld went on to lead the Southeastern Conference in scoring at 25.3 points per game. King finished second at 25.2 and repeated as the league's player of the year. He also recorded the most improbable basket in program history. Appropriately enough he produced it at his favorite venue, Rupp Arena in Lexington.

Down by 12 points with three minutes left, Tennessee rallied furiously to tie the score and force overtime. Early in the extra period, King leaped high to grab an inbounds pass. Off-balance when he landed, he heaved the ball toward the basket while falling onto his back. Big Blue fans watched with a mixture of dismay and disbelief as the spectacular shot went in, spurring the Volunteers to a 90–88 victory.

Tennessee finished the 1975–76 regular season with a 21–5 record and a number twelve national ranking, but fate was about to kick the Big Orange in the teeth. King injured his right hand during preparations for the NCAA Tournament and watched from the bench as the Volunteers suffered a season-ending 81–75 upset loss to Virginia Military Institute. In spite of that gut-wrenching setback, Mears figured 1976–77 could be a national championship season for the Volunteers. With Grunfeld and King teaming up for the third and final time, the headman knew one thing: It was now or never.

As the Ernie and Bernie Show opened the final season of its remarkable run, even casual observers were struck by the stark contrast in the two young men. Easygoing and sociable, Grunfeld routinely chatted with officials and opponents. Clearly he viewed basketball as a friendly competition. Conversely King exhibited a controlled rage on the court, glaring at opponents with a contempt that defies description. As Grunfeld once noted, "He just looks like he hates the other guy."

Just Call Him "Burger"

Tennessee teammates of the 1970s quickly discovered Bernard King had a knack for nonconformity and a fondness for hamburgers. One time the talented New Yorker stopped the team bus in downtown Nashville, stepped off just long enough to buy two double-A batteries for his tape player, then returned to the bus and jammed the rest of the ride.

Another time King showed up for a team meeting with a burger and french fries, munching his lunch while head coach Ray Mears held court. Normally a strict disciplinarian, Mears allowed the incident to pass without comment.

Finally, on a road trip to play the University of Kentucky, the team bus stopped at a fine restaurant in Berea. A picture of elegance, Boone Tavern featured antique tables, linen napkins, and fancy fare such as lamb chops and baked salmon. King scanned the menu, saw nothing that appealed to him, and then stunned the waitstaff by ordering a hamburger. Service was delayed quite some time while a tavern employee drove to the nearest fast-food spot to fill King's order.

Given Bernard's taste for ground beef, you wonder why no one ever gave him a suitable nickname. Then again, "Burger" King might have sparked all kinds of legal complications.

Bernard King was a virtual scoring machine during his years at Tennessee.

King may have hated his opponents, but he loved to score. Few players in the game's history have done so with more grace and skill. As a freshman King once asked Mears to be excused from team drills so he could practice his post moves on the opposite end of the court. The headman reluctantly agreed, then watched in amazement as King worked and worked and worked. "I had never seen a guy work as hard on offensive moves," Mears said later. "He knew more about what he needed than we did."

In addition to incredible quickness and an unsurpassed work ethic, King had an uncanny knack for improvisation. Even he struggled to explain it. "Ninety percent of what I do is planned," he once said. "The other 10 percent, I don't know where it comes from. But when it comes, those are the big, big nights."

Like King, Grunfeld was driven by a relentless desire to be the best. "You don't really coach Ernie," Aberdeen noted. "You just point him in the right direction and say, 'We need a basket.' He'll get one for you."

All but lost in the Ernie and Bernie hoopla was the fact they had a top-notch supporting cast. Johnny Darden was a dazzling ball handler who triggered the fast break. Reggie Johnson was a freshman post player who would go on to distinguish himself in the National Basketball Association. The other starter, Mike Jackson, was an exceptional guard who started for three years and averaged 14 points per game for his college career. "There must be a hundred teams in this country that I could lead in scoring," Jackson said during his senior season. "I might even be an All-American. But I don't think much about it, because I like what I'm doing and I know my role."

King's role, meanwhile, was full-time superstar and part-time problem child. Assorted off-the-court problems earned him an

Grunfeld (left) and King graced the cover of Sports Illustrated *magazine in 1976.*

early-season suspension and led to a couple of early-season losses. The Vols regrouped, however, to win their next twelve games in a row, including a stirring 71–67 upset of second-ranked Kentucky in Lexington.

Tennessee carried a 20–5 record and a number seven national ranking into March but needed to beat Kentucky and

Vanderbilt at home to clinch a tie for the Southeastern Conference title. King willed the Big Orange past the Big Blue (81–79) for the fifth consecutive time, then the Volunteers dumped Vandy 65–55 to lock up a share of the league championship and a second consecutive NCAA Tournament bid.

Shortly thereafter King collected his third consecutive Southeastern Conference Player of the Year award and his second league scoring title.

Grunfeld, runner-up in the scoring race, shared player of the year recognition. Both were tabbed All-America.

Still Tennessee's NCAA Tournament jinx continued. Both King and Grunfeld fouled out as the Volunteers suffered a 93–88 overtime loss to Syracuse in first-round play. With Grunfeld out of eligibility, King opted to bypass his senior year at Tennessee in favor of the National Basketball Association draft. Both were first-round picks. Grunfeld enjoyed a decent career, but King developed into a dominating player. He earned all-star recognition three times and led the league in scoring one year at 32.9 points per game.

Inextricably linked in college, King and Grunfeld saw fate bring them back together as members of the New York Knicks from 1982 to 1986. Even now—nearly thirty years after they played their final college game—they are the two most famous names in Tennessee basketball history. A 24,500-seat on-campus arena stands as a testament to the level of popularity Vol hoops achieved during their tenure. The official name is Thompson-Boling Arena. But longtime Vol fans know it as "The House Ernie and Bernie Built."

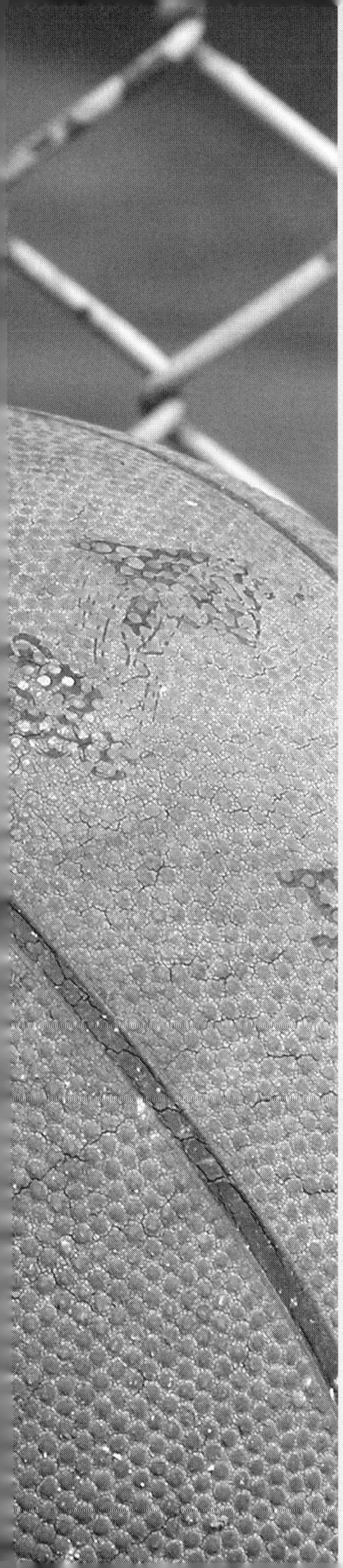

Taming the Wildcats

When Xavier used a time-out called by Tennessee's Don DeVoe to set up a last-second basket that beat the Big Orange 51–50 in the finals of the 1978 Volunteer Classic, disgruntled fans heaped verbal abuse on their first-year head coach. Still stinging from the barbs when his team gathered on the practice floor two days later, DeVoe approached junior guard Bert Bertelkamp, who had missed a technical foul shot in the final three minutes of play. "You know, Bert," DeVoe wisecracked, "if you hadn't missed that technical foul shot, I wouldn't be dealing with all this heat."

Grinning smugly the unflappable Bertelkamp replied, "If you hadn't called that time-out, you wouldn't be dealing with all this heat."

DeVoe's response? "I can't repeat what he said," Bertelkamp recalled years later, "but I can tell you this: He wasn't amused."

DeVoe was even less amused when Knoxville's newspapers spent the next week reprinting letters from irate readers questioning his coaching ability. In desperation he telephoned one of the local sports editors to seek an end to the criticism. When no relief was forthcoming, DeVoe wondered if he'd made a mistake by leaving a secure job at the University of Wyoming to accept the reins at Tennessee. It seemed he had inherited a coach's nightmare.

To begin with, the program he assumed was coming off an 11–16 record in 1977–78 that included a dismal 6–12 Southeastern Conference mark. The team had played no defense—losing by 121–87 and 101–86 scores to Louisiana State and dropping the season finale 107–94 at Auburn. The squad's best athlete, Terry Crosby, was known for turnovers and poor shot selection. The program's best post defender, sophomore forward Howard Wood, was so grossly out of shape that he was banned from practice until he lost thirty-five pounds. And the team's most experienced player, flashy point guard Johnny Darden, found DeVoe's deliberate offense so confining that he lost his cool and his first-team job.

Further complicating the picture was the fact the new coach was making Tennessee switch from zone defense to man-to-man and from a star system to an all-for-one approach. "Ray Mears had promoted stars," DeVoe recalls. "I wanted to focus on the team, but the players had not been recruited to adhere to that philosophy. For a guy like Darden, who had been captain the year before and expected to step into star status, it was difficult when he found out he wasn't going to get that kind of emphasis."

Essentially the Volunteers of 1978–79 were long on self-esteem and short on self-discipline. Even school president Ed Boling conceded as much during a chat with the new coach. "I talked to some school officials in preseason, and they just weren't impressed with the kids we had," DeVoe recalled. "Dr. Boling, in particular, felt we'd be lucky to get the guys to play hard and play together." Somehow, though, DeVoe got the Vols to do just that. The result was a memorable season that included not one, not two, but three victories over defending national champ Kentucky.

First, however, DeVoe would make a few enemies. Shortly after taking the job, he alienated a bunch of fans by announcing he was putting the gaudy orange blazers worn by predecessors Ray Mears and Cliff Wettig in mothballs. He alienated several more by scrapping the fast-break attack in favor of a slower-tempo half-court offense. Then he alienated still more fans by calling that controversial time-out in the title game of the Volunteer Classic.

Tennessee generally captured its own holiday tournament with relative ease. But December 17, 1978, found the Vols

Just Bite Your Tongue

Operating on the premise that athletes should be seen and not heard, Tennessee coach Don DeVoe was especially intolerant of basketball players who complained to the officials.

Certainly DeVoe had no qualms about baiting officials. He knew a timely technical foul could motivate his players, ignite a listless crowd, and ensure a favorable ruling on the next borderline call. What worried him were the *untimely* technicals, the kind hot-tempered players tended to incur at crucial points in a game. DeVoe took forceful steps to make sure this didn't happen to one of his athletes. "If one of us got a technical foul, everybody had to run," Bert Bertelkamp recalls.

There were no exceptions to this rule, as the Vols learned two months into DeVoe's first season at the helm. One of Tennessee's players was whistled for a technical in a game at Vanderbilt on Saturday night, January 22, 1979. The Vols hung on to win 71–70, then flew to Baton Rouge, site of their next game. They arrived at the team hotel in the wee hours of Sunday morning, but that didn't stop DeVoe from assembling them a few hours later—not at Louisiana State University's gym, but at the school track.

"One of our guys had gotten a technical Saturday night, so Coach DeVoe had us run eight laps around LSU's track at six the next morning," Bertelkamp recalls. "It was pouring down rain, but that didn't matter. We still had to run."

leading unheralded Xavier by a 50–49 margin with mere seconds remaining. The crisis appeared to pass when Xavier missed a potential game-winning shot, but Reggie Johnson fumbled the rebound out of bounds, giving the visitors one more chance. "I felt we had to get our defense set, so I called time-out," DeVoe realls. "You defend from the basket outward, so I wanted to make sure Xavier didn't get anything in close."

The strategy was sound, but the visitors didn't follow the script. "They got the ball to a key player, and he knocked down the shot with one second to go," DeVoe says, still annoyed a quarter-century later. "It was a pretty darned long shot but the guy made it."

The game-winning shot was a low-percentage rainbow from deep in the corner, but that didn't matter to angry Vol fans. Many of them roasted DeVoe for calling a time-out they felt gave Xavier additional time set up the final shot. Basically it was a damned-if-you-do, damned-if-you-don't situation.

"I've thought many times since then that I wish I hadn't called that time-out," DeVoe says. "But if you don't call a time-out and the opponent gets an easy shot, you second-guess yourself for that. During your career you have a few of those that go for you and few that go against you." When this one went against him, DeVoe found many Volunteer fans turning against him. Fortunately, he and his team were about to launch a rally that would make them the toast of Tennessee.

The Volunteers stood 10–6 overall and 3–2 in Southeastern Conference play when they showed up in Lexington to face tradition-rich Kentucky on January 20, 1979. "I felt really comfortable going into the game," DeVoe recalls. "November and

Coach Don DeVoe brought a lot of fire to the Volunteer bench.

December weren't strong months for us, but the pieces were falling into place in January."

Originally signed as a shooting guard, Bertelkamp had moved to point guard and eventually wrested the first-team job from Darden. Bertelkamp, a Knoxville native who fancied himself more of a scorer after averaging 11 points per game as a sophomore, found the move a little disappointing. Darden, who had started the previous three seasons, found the move virtually intolerable.

"Johnny Darden had been point guard for three years, but he was more used to an upbeat, fast-break style of play," Bertelkamp recalls. "That didn't fit with the way Coach DeVoe wanted to play, so Johnny got bumped out, Gary Carter came in at the wing, and I moved to the point. I was happy to be playing, but I wasn't thrilled to be playing point guard, because it wasn't my best position. The Southeastern Conference had a lot of quick point guards, and they would really come after me because I didn't have the quickness Darden did to just blow past them. It worked out, though."

Indeed it did. By midseason, Bertelkamp was growing comfortable in his new role. "Bert did a great job directing the offense," DeVoe says. "It was tough on Darden, who had been a three-year starter, but Bertelkamp was giving me the direction I wanted at point guard."

That direction was evident on January 20, when the Vols invaded Rupp Arena to face Kentucky. Johnson picked up his third foul just eight seconds into the second half but played cautiously enough thereafter to avoid fouling out. Wood picked up his fourth moments later and gave way to Kevin Nash, a 6'10" sophomore.

Tennessee led comfortably for much of the game, but Kentucky closed to 59–53 with 3:30 remaining. Nash rammed home a dunk off a nice assist from Carter, however, and the Big Blue's comeback was dead in the water. "Kentucky is the loudest place you've ever been until the fans realize they're going to lose," Bertelkamp recalled. "Then it's quiet as a morgue."

Tennessee's 66–55 victory provided just the boost the sluggish Volunteers needed. "That was our first big win, and it gave the team a whole lot of confidence," Bertelkamp said. "We had no problem getting the ball inside to big guys, Reggie Johnson in particular. We had this play, number seven, and we ran it over and over and over. We'd get the ball to Reggie on the block and he was able to score most of the time."

Johnson finished with 20 points. Nash chipped in 10 points and "did a monumental job with his rebounding," according to DeVoe. Of Carter, the coach said, "Everything you'd want a senior to do Gary Carter is doing as a freshman."

Although beating Kentucky in Lexington was a rare feat, DeVoe seemed surprisingly calm. Recalling that Louisville had crushed Tennessee on an earlier visit to the Bluegrass State, Bertelkamp looked up at his head coach and said, "This was a lot better than our last trip to Kentucky."

"I expected to come up here and beat Kentucky," DeVoe matter of factly replied.

Bertelkamp was stunned. "Prior to that game in Lexington, we hadn't beaten anybody any good in two years," he recalls. "But Don didn't see it as that big a deal. "

DeVoe says he simply chose to keep the victory in perspective. "They had graduated five or six outstanding players off their

Bert Bertelkamp helped direct three defeats of Kentucky.

national title team of the year before," he recalled, "and they were still in the throes of finding themselves. We were playing really solid basketball, and they never really made a strong run at us."

Following the win in Lexington, the Big Orange split its next eight games. Thus Tennessee stood 15–10 overall and 8–6 in league play when the Big Blue visited Knoxville on February 17. The rematch proved to be even more one-sided than the earlier meeting. Johnson picked up three fouls in the game's first four minutes, took a seat on the bench, then returned for roughly a minute before being whistled for foul number four. With the score tied at 25–all, Kentucky was poised to exploit Johnson's absence. It never did, though; Vol reserves came through like champions.

Nash, rapidly developing a reputation as a Wildcat killer, came off the bench to hit 11 quick points before spraining his ankle after being pushed by a Big Blue defender. "That really ticked me off when Kev got hurt," Wood said. "With Reggie on the bench with four fouls and Kev gone with that ankle, the rest of us knew we just had to play harder." And that's precisely what they did. In retrospect, the injury to Nash may have been the worst thing that happened to the Wildcats all night. "We're a very emotional team," Crosby said. "With Kev hurt, we knew we had to score more points."

As things turned out, the Vols scored plenty. When Wood was tagged with his fourth foul just five minutes into the second half, Tennessee was reduced to playing 6'6" Chuck Threeths and 6'4" Steve Ray at the post positions. It didn't matter, though. Crosby (23 points) and Carter (19) picked up the slack as the Big Orange hammered the Big Blue 101–84.

Most observers were surprised by the severity of the beating. Not Bertelkamp. "We felt we had Kentucky's number," he recalls. "They set a lot of on-the-ball picks for [All-American] Kyle Macy, but we cut him off; if you did that, you could stop Kentucky. We just had more talent and athleticism that year than they did. Joe B. Hall never did very well in Knoxville. Even when he had better talent, his teams didn't seem to play well at Stokely Center. They seemed to play tight."

The loss was Kentucky's worst since a 98–74 setback to Indiana five years earlier. Even the normally reserved DeVoe was beaming after the victory, calling it "one of the truly remarkable games in my short career."

Speaking of remarkable accomplishments, Crosby produced one play that even his coach still finds unbelievable and inconceivable. "Terry made a play that night that I've never seen another player make," DeVoe says. "He had just scored a basket and was starting back down the floor. When the Kentucky center took the ball out of bounds, Terry instinctively whirled around, intercepted the inbounds pass, and laid the ball in for another basket."

Spurred by their annihilation of the Wildcats, the Volunteers upset nineteenth-ranked Vanderbilt two days later and then posted road wins at Florida and Auburn to finish the regular season on a six-game winning streak. Best of all their 12–6 conference record earned them a number two seeding for the league tournament, which was being resuscitated after a twenty-five-year absence. "We were fortunate in that the Southeastern Conference seeded the first- and second-place teams into the tournament semifinals," DeVoe recalls. "Everybody else had to play two games before we played our first one."

When the Vols bounced Auburn 75–64 in their semifinal test, they found themselves advancing to the finals. Their opponent was Kentucky, which had upset Louisiana State in the other semifinal game. "We were happy to be playing Kentucky instead of LSU," Bertelkamp recalls. "We only beat LSU one time in my four years at Tennessee; they had our number, much like we had Kentucky's number."

For a while the Wildcats seemed to have changed their number. Needing the tournament title to earn an NCAA Tournament bid, the Big Blue clawed its way to a 44–37 halftime lead. DeVoe spent the break challenging his team to tighten up its defense and turn up its intensity. The Vols did as instructed, holding Kentucky scoreless for the first seven minutes of the second half on their way to grabbing a 45–44 lead. "We went to our full-court dynamite press," DeVoe recalled afterward. "We forced the backcourt turnovers, and we converted. Then we made Kentucky play our tempo after we got the lead." Tennessee's defense was so stifling that the Wildcats attempted just four shots over the game's final 8:20. The Vols weren't hitting their shots, however, and regulation play ended with the score tied at 55–all.

The Big Orange offense began to click in overtime. Threeths, Johnson, and Carter hit free throws as the Vols surged in front 61–55. Crosby and Woods hit field goals, then Carter sank four consecutive free throws and a transition layup as the lead widened to 71–63. The final score was 75–69.

Carter paced the Vols with 22 points. Crosby added 14 points while limiting Macy, the tournament's most valuable player, to 10. "Gary Carter played a tremendous game," Bertelkamp

Terry Crosby (25) became one of the Southeastern Conference's premier players.

Howard Wood was a key player for the 1978–79 Vols.

recalls. "And Crosby did a fantastic job guarding Macy, as usual. It was a big win, but we were not surprised to beat 'em that third time. We had no fear of Kentucky. We were never intimidated by them."

DeVoe wasn't intimidated, either. But having grown up in neighboring Ohio, he knew Big Blue basketball was something special. "I was aware of the prestige of the Kentucky basketball program, so beating them three times in one season was incredible," he says. "I felt we had every advantage, though. They were still putting their team together after losing so many standouts from the previous year. And they had to play four games in four days, whereas we only had to play two games in two days."

Regardless the third defeat of Kentucky was Tennessee's biggest because it gave DeVoe a league tournament title in his first year as the Volunteers coach. "It was like a dream come true," he says. "So many people felt like the guys would not be able to come together and play as well as they did. But they came together for me. To this day I don't think I ever had better wing play than I got from Crosby and Carter that year. Those two kids laid it on the line for me."

The supporting cast played exceptionally well, too. "Bertelkamp did a great job at point," DeVoe notes. "Howard Wood, Reggie Johnson, Kevin Nash, and Chuck Threeths played well on the inside, and Steve Ray came off the bench to provide a spark. The key to that season was everybody coming together and playing their roles."

That included Darden, who bit his tongue and swallowed his pride after going from team captain as a junior to reserve status as a senior. "I don't think it's ever easy to accept being supplanted by another player after you've been a team leader," DeVoe says. "But Darden eventually learned to accept his role."

Looking back on a year filled with pleasant surprises, DeVoe recalls one that stands above the rest: "Terry Crosby," he says. "He was a marvelous athlete, but a lot of people told me he was an uncoachable kid . . . that he'd had his way for so long that it would be hard to get him to accept what I was teaching. But he really turned it on for me. I just regret that I never had another year to coach him."

Another classic success story was Wood, whose playing time and productivity increased as his waistline decreased. "Woody was just a chunky kid when he reported," DeVoe says. "I wouldn't let him practice with the team until he lost thirty-five pounds. [Trainer] Mike Rollo had to virtually live with him and starve him because he was eating himself out of a scholarship. But Woody turned out to be one of the real keys to the season."

Ultimately the 1978–79 season saw Tennessee finish 21–12, claim the league tournament title, and notch the first NCAA Tournament victory in program history. Still veteran Vol fans will always remember that season as the one that saw a rookie coach hand mighty Kentucky three memorable defeats.

"The year before, we played zone defense; we weren't going to stop you, we were going to outscore you," Bertelkamp recalls. "But Coach DeVoe was able to sell us on man-to-man defense. We beat Kentucky three times and won the SEC Tournament with the same team—plus Gary Carter—that had a losing record the year before. It was pretty obvious Coach DeVoe was the big reason."

Not surprisingly the headman's popularity soared. And that little incident at the end of the Xavier game? Heck, it was all but forgotten.

Five Years, Five Bids

Don DeVoe thought he had seen everything. But this was a new experience. Normally as focused as a horse wearing blinders, Tennessee's ultra-intense head coach found his concentration divided as he paced the sidelines at the Murphy Center in Murfreesboro on March 9, 1979. Lifting his gaze from pregame warm-ups, he scanned the jam-packed arena. An amazing number of orange-clad fans had crammed into the gym and were shouting encouragement while beating the air with orange and white shakers.

Even in the tension of this nerve-wracking pre–tip-off moment, DeVoe was touched. "We had 99 percent of arena filled with Tennessee fans and more outside trying to get in," he recalled, still moved by the memory twenty-five years later. "That was the most incredible thing—seeing that level of excitement for Tennessee basketball. That game was the highlight of the year for me."

Several factors combined to make that evening extra special:

- This was an NCAA Tournament game.
- This was a Cinderella team that had greatly exceeded expectations.
- This was a game being played in the Volunteer State, which accounted for the decidedly pro-Tennessee crowd.
- This was a setting that produced the first NCAA Tournament victory in the program's seventy-year history.

Amazingly Tennessee's first sixty-nine years of intercollegiate basketball competition produced hundreds of memorable moments but zero wins in "The Big Dance." That trend appeared likely to continue when the keyed-up Volunteers committed turnovers on their first three possessions and fell behind Eastern Kentucky 15–5 in the first round of the 1979 Mideast Regional. The assembled Vol boosters watched anxiously and waited eagerly, hoping for a reason to cheer. They were about to get one.

Freshman Gary Carter scored three quick baskets to ignite a rally that Terry Crosby fueled with three more buckets. By half-

Don DeVoe guided the Vols to their first ever NCAA Tournament victory.

time the Volunteers carried a 44–38 advantage and a ton of momentum.

Star forward Reggie Johnson went to the bench with his fourth foul early in the second half, but the Big Orange, seemingly oblivious to his absence, immediately parlayed a 10–2 spurt into a 64–52 lead with 13:28 remaining. The differential peaked at 22 points, as the Big Orange went on to prevail 97–81. The celebration began just as Tennessee's NCAA Tournament futility ended. "We made history," Vol reserve Chuck Threeths beamed. "We did it!"

Even DeVoe, whose demeanor generally ranged from low-key to stoic, was uncharacteristically bubbly. "It was inconceivable to me that Tennessee, with all of the success it had experienced to that point, had never won an NCAA Tournament game," he said. "It meant everything to the program, the players, and our loyal fans."

After permitting himself several minutes of semi-elation, however, DeVoe returned to his usual ultradignified demeanor. "This game was won in the final eight minutes of the first half," he said. "By getting the ball to Terry Crosby, we were able to turn it around, going from a 10-point deficit to a 44–38 halftime lead. In the first ten minutes, we played very poorly, but our kids snapped out of it; and in the second half the game was entirely Tennessee's."

Junior guard Bert Bertelkamp, looking back a quarter-century later, recalls that milestone victory as "a tremendous accomplishment. People said before the season that our talent level wasn't very good; I never believed that. Terry Crosby was a tremendous athlete who, if he'd had another year under Don DeVoe, would've played ten years in the NBA. Reggie Johnson was a great offensive player who had a nice pro career, and Gary Carter turned out to be a better player than expected. We were proud of ourselves, because people thought we were a bunch of losers."

Johnson led the Vols with 20 points. Crosby added 19 and Carter 18, as Tennessee won its ninth game in a row, improved its record to 21–11, and earned the berth opposite fifth-ranked Notre Dame in the region semifinals. Two days later the Big Orange returned to the Murphy Center and found another packed house of Vol fanatics waiting. "We got great support," Bertelkamp said. "We found out there are a lot of Tennessee fans all over the state, not just in Knoxville. Tennessee's a football school, but fans will support basketball if the team's good."

And—make no mistake—this Tennessee team was *very* good. The Vols played the Irish dead-even for twenty minutes, going to halftime tied at 32. Notre Dame coach Digger Phelps opened the second half with a full-court press, however, and Tennessee failed to get the ball across midcourt on its first three possessions. The Irish converted each turnover into points, fueling a 14–4 spurt that produced a 46–36 lead.

Tennessee rallied, but its comeback died when Johnson fouled out with 5:38 left and the Vols trailing 56–51. They would get no closer, ultimately losing 73–67. Still, DeVoe had reason to smile. The first-year coach had taken a team pegged for mediocrity in preseason to a 21–12 record, second place in the Southeastern Conference regular-season standings, first place in the league tournament, and its first-ever NCAA Tournament triumph. "This has been a glorious year for the University of Tennessee basketball team," he said. "Coming from the middle of the pack to win the Southeastern Conference Tournament,

Just Your Basic Miracle Finish

Moments after missing a jump shot that left Tennessee trailing American University 58–57 on December 18, 1981, Gary Carter stood near midcourt and watched as fans filed glumly toward the exits. Glancing at the clock, which showed just three seconds remaining, he had no idea he was about to make the most spectacular play in Stokely Athletics Center history.

The Eagles' Mark Nickens needed only to inbound the ball to a teammate to kill the final three seconds and seal the victory. Knowing this, all five Tennessee players positioned themselves on American's end of the floor to try and deny the inbounds pass.

Seeing teammate Ed Sloane temporarily break free, Nickens fired a hard pass in his direction. Carter alertly stepped in front to intercept, then turned and heaved the ball toward the basket. The shot hit nothing but nylon on its way through the hoop, making Carter a hero and making Tennessee a dramatic 59–58 victor.

Although he finished with 22 points, Carter scored just 2 second-half points prior to his buzzer-beating bomb. After missing his next-to-last shot, leaving American University ahead by a point, he figured the Vols doom was sealed. "It was looking slim," he said. "They had to make a stupid foul or throw the ball away. A miracle had to happen."

It did.

Gary Carter (left) going after a rebound against Auburn.

TENNES
14
25

beating Kentucky three times, and Vanderbilt and Alabama twice each . . . these are things we'll never forget about the season."

Even the season-ending loss to Notre Dame produced a victory on the recruiting front. The passion of the assembled Volunteer fans made a powerful impression on a young prospect who watched the action from courtside. His name was Dale Ellis, and he was destined to become one of the greatest players in Tennessee history. "If ever there was a game a prospect should see, it was that one," DeVoe recalls. "We had all the fans, even though it wasn't a home game, and that enabled us to recruit Dale Ellis. He came on board and he really helped us."

Indeed. The 6'7" Ellis would help Tennessee reach the next four NCAA Tournaments, giving the program an unprecedented five consecutive bids.

Bid number two, however, was tricky, because the 1979–80 Vols were a streaky bunch. They opened the season with a 97–80 blowout of ninth-ranked St. John's, then lost to number fourteen Louisville 77–75. After five wins in a row, they lost back-to-back games to second-ranked Ohio State (91–65) and tenth-ranked Indiana (70–68). The Vols won their next six, improving to 12–3, then lost their next five, falling to 12–8. Tennessee won five of its final six regular-season games but lost to Ole Miss in round one of the Southeastern Conference Tournament.

With a modest 17–10 overall record, the Big Orange was barely "on the bubble" for an NCAA Tournament bid. Bertelkamp figured the bubble was destined to burst. "We were sweating it," he recalls. "Frankly I didn't think we were going to get in."

Dale Ellis (14) guided Tennessee to four NCAA tournaments.

He was so sure, in fact, he neglected to watch the national telecast of the NCAA Tournament pairings. Later that evening he got a surprise phone call from his father. "You got in," said Hank Bertelkamp, who had played for the basketball Vols two decades earlier. "I just saw it on TV."

His son still couldn't believe Tennessee was going back to The Big Dance. "I thought my father was talking about the Commissioner's Tournament," Bert recalled, referring to a short-lived affair for teams that barely missed the NCAA field.

DeVoe wasn't nearly as surprised. "Our 17–10 record wasn't spectacular, but it came against some of the best teams in the country," he said. "Our schedule was ranked number one in the country that year, and I think strength of schedule was a big factor in our getting a bid."

Whatever the reason, the Vols were going back to The Dance. This time their first-round game would be played in Greensboro, North Carolina, against a scrappy Furman team known for its stingy man-to-man defense. Electing to go with quickness over size, DeVoe replaced 6'10" Kevin Nash and 6'7" Ellis with 6'6" Threeths and 6'4" Steve Ray. The ploy worked, helping Tennessee roll to a 40–29 halftime lead. The Paladins closed to 48–41 with 15:41 to go, but Wood scored six consecutive points, and the crisis passed. Johnson finished with 28 points and Wood 19, as the Volunteers prevailed 80–69.

Johnson's brilliance continued in the second-round game against eighth-ranked Maryland. He scored 17 points in the first fourteen minutes as the Vols raced to a 29–18 lead. Johnson

Reggie Johnson (32) going high for the score.

33
URGIA
3

scored two more buckets in the opening minutes of the second half and appeared on his way to a career day. Then, with the Vols leading 46–39, he was whistled for two fouls—his third and fourth of the game—within a span of ten seconds. When he went to the bench, Tennessee's upset hopes went with him. The Terrapins dominated thereafter, eventually winning 86–75. "Reggie Johnson was playing great, and we had the game in tow," DeVoe recalled. "Then they called those quick fouls on him, and we lost the momentum. That was a really disappointing loss."

Generally reluctant to criticize officials, the Vol coach made an exception in this case. "I guarantee you we got the short end of the officiating in the second half," DeVoe said. "You don't win in tournament play when you get the short end. The two fouls on Johnson were the turning point."

Bertelkamp, who had dished out a career-best 16 assists in his final collegiate game, was even harsher in his assessment of the officials. He hinted there was an ulterior motive, promoting the basketball-crazed Atlantic Coast Conference. "An ACC school—I believe it was North Carolina—had lost earlier in the day," he recalls, "and we heard people say that the NCAA couldn't afford to have no ACC schools in the tournament. We could've beaten Maryland, because they couldn't stop Reggie. When they blew those two fouls on him at the start of the second half, that was it for us."

That was it for 1980, all right, but the Vols would be back in March of 1981 for their third consecutive NCAA Tournament experience. And this time they were loaded for bear.

Despite the departure of Johnson and Bertelkamp, Tennessee had come out smoking in 1980–81. The Volunteers won thirteen of their first fifteen games and achieved a number eight national ranking. "That was an interesting season, because we had to bring some new players on board, and we really had to step it up," DeVoe recalls. "Dale Ellis was emerging as one of the premier inside players in the country, and two freshmen—Michael Brooks and Tyrone Beaman—were really outstanding guards."

Still the Vols' inexperience in the backcourt began to show at season's end; they lost two of their last three regular-season games and then dropped their Southeastern Conference Tournament opener to Ole Miss. Still the Big Orange carried a 20–7 record, a number fifteen national ranking, and high hopes into the NCAA Tournament's East Regional.

Following a first-round bye, Tennessee rolled into Charlotte, North Carolina, to face a red-hot Virginia Commonwealth squad that was riding a sixteen-game winning streak. Tennessee raced to a 14-point lead and led by 13 (38–25) early in the second half. Then the Big Orange got careless, enabling the Rams to seize the momentum. Danny Kottak capped a frantic rally with a bucket that tied the game 56–56 with 2:24 left. Tennessee held for the final shot, but Ellis disdained a 15-foot jumper in favor of an ill-advised pass that squandered the Vols' last possession of regulation.

Overtime provided considerably more tension than action. After getting the tip, Virginia Commonwealth elected to hold the ball until it got a wide-open shot. When Tennessee's defense wouldn't permit one, however, the Rams eventually lost possession on a turnover. The Vols then decided *they* would hold the ball for a wide-open shot. When it wasn't forthcoming, DeVoe called time-out with 19 seconds left to set up a play designed to get the ball to Howard Wood. "The ball was supposed to come to me, and I was supposed to pass it to Howard in the corner," Ellis recalled. "It was Howard that kept us in the game, and it's usually him who takes the final shot."

Not this time, though. Brooks passed the ball to Ellis at the free throw line, the same spot he'd been when he passed up the potential game-winning shot at the end of regulation. This time, seeing Wood covered, Ellis unloaded a 16-footer that swished through the rim a split-second before the final horn sounded. "I don't think there's been a bigger shot in Tennessee basketball in a long time than the one Dale Ellis made," said DeVoe, a man not given to hyperbole.

That point might have been debatable, but this much was not: The Vols' next challenge would be the biggest—or at least *tallest*—in program history: 7'4" Ralph Sampson and the fifth-ranked Virginia Cavaliers. Asked following the Virginia Commonwealth game how he felt about the prospect of guarding a man 9 inches taller than him, Tennessee's 6'7" Howard Wood replied, "I haven't really thought about it." Asked when he would think about it, the rugged Volunteer quipped, "In about five minutes."

Tennessee was a decided underdog when it showed up for the Mideast Region finals in Atlanta, but the Volunteers were not intimidated by Sampson or Virginia. Perhaps playing a little over their heads, they forged a 36–31 lead early in the second half. "I thought, 'We got 'em . . . we got 'em on the ropes,'" Wood said. "And if we keep playing consistent for the next seven or eight minutes, we can go into our stall."

The only thing consistent about the Vols thereafter, however, was their inconsistency. With Tennessee's defense collapsing on Sampson, who was limited to one second-half point, Jeff Lamp ignited a 27–4 Virginia explosion that spurred the Cavaliers to a

62–48 triumph. "They had a great player who took control, made the great plays," Brooks said of Lamp. "If he hadn't taken control at that point, they wouldn't have won."

Despite a sizable height disadvantage, Ellis proved to be surprisingly effective around the basket. The Vol standout outscored Sampson 13 points to 9 and outrebounded him 9 to 5. "Hell, Ralph Sampson was 9 inches taller than Dale," DeVoe noted, "but even he couldn't take Dale out of his shooting style."

Tennessee's decision to pack its defense around Sampson provided mixed results. It limited the towering Cavalier to 4-of-13 shooting but enabled his teammates to hit twenty of thirty attempts. "Virginia was just really strong," DeVoe recalls. "It went to the Final Four that year."

But, as fate would have it, the Vols and Cavaliers would be meeting again the same time next year.

With only Wood missing from the year before, Tennessee opened the 1981–82 season with a loss at Purdue, followed by five consecutive wins. Then DeVoe got the worst Christmas surprise of his life. On December 24 starting guards Gary Carter and Ed Littleton were ruled academically ineligible. The loss of the former was especially hurtful. "Carter was playing his best basketball ever—averaging 20 points per game, shooting 55 percent from the field, and developing into a great player," DeVoe noted. "He was going to be an All-American that year. Losing those two players really hurt the team's momentum."

That's for sure. The Vols lost two of their next three games and saw their record dip to 6–3. With the rugged Southeastern Conference portion of the schedule about to begin, Tennessee's season appeared headed for oblivion. Even the head coach was engulfed in pessimism. "When I got the news on Christmas eve that Gary and Ed would not be readmitted for the winter quarter, I figured it would be tough to have a winning season," DeVoe said. "I didn't think we had the firepower to compete in this league, and I put it to the team to prove me wrong."

That's precisely what happened. The shorthanded Vols did something no one could have expected: They jelled. Sinking 16 consecutive shots at one stretch, Tennessee hammered twelfth-ranked Alabama 88–67. Then the Vols shot a sizzling 75 percent from the floor in a 62–55 defeat of Ole Miss in Oxford. The hot shooting continued, as they stretched their winning streak to eight games. All of a sudden the Big Orange had a 14–3 record, including a league-leading 9–0 conference mark. "My feet haven't touched the ground in four weeks," DeVoe said. "I'm totally surprised at what we've accomplished."

Part of the credit belonged to Brooks and Beaman, who were rapidly growing into the roles previously held by Carter and Littleton. "They were playing like gangbusters," DeVoe said.

A bigger part of Tennessee's success, however, could be traced to Ellis's emergence as one of the country's premier players. "I've never had a player to play as well as Dale has this year," DeVoe said. "He's been outstanding in all phases of the game—scoring, rebounding, defensively. I think when we lost Carter and Littleton, he took it upon himself not to let us collapse."

The Vols never collapsed, but they stumbled a bit. Three losses in a row—two of them in overtime—suggested the league had caught up with Tennessee. But, having come this far, the Vols weren't about to give up their title hopes. A four-game winning streak got them back on track, and they finished regular-season play 18–8 and tied for the Southeastern Conference top spot at 13–5. No one was more surprised by these accomplishments than DeVoe, who noted, "It was incredible that we were able to come along that well after losing Carter and Littleton."

After splitting two games in the league tournament, Tennessee accepted its fourth consecutive NCAA Tournament bid. Meanwhile, DeVoe accepted the Southeastern Conference's Coach of the Year award and Ellis the league's Player of the Year award.

Seeded ninth, Tennessee drew eighth-seeded Southwest Louisiana in round one of the Mideast Regional at Indianapolis. The Ragin' Cajuns gave the Vols fits, trailing just 51–49 entering the final minutes. But Ellis hit two free throws and a jump shot to give Tennessee a 55–49 lead, then Brooks sealed a 61–57 victory by sinking 6 free throws in the final minute. "The key was having the lead going into the final five minutes," a relieved DeVoe said afterward. "We had our best foul shooters in the game, and we kept the ball in the best man's hands."

Those words would prove painfully ironic two days later. Drawing Virginia as its second-round foe a second year in succession, the Vols scratched and clawed their way to a 38–28 lead early in the second half. As the game entered the home stretch, however, the unthinkable happened. The Big Orange missed four of five free throws in the last 3:12. Three of the misfires—including one by Brooks—came on the front end of one-and-ones, and those six potential points proved decisive as the Big Orange bowed 54–51. Brooks (24) and Ellis (16) combined to score all but 11 of Tennessee's points.

Terry Holland, coach of the third-ranked Cavaliers, saluted the fallen Vols for their gritty effort. "The shame about the NCAA

Tournament," he said, "is that a team can give a great effort and leave its guts out on the floor, like Tennessee did, and still not advance."

Ellis found no consolation in such talk. "We had the game under control," he noted. "All we had to do was hit free throws." Ellis, however, would get one more chance at The Big Dance.

After sweeping their first eight games, the 1982–83 Vols went 9–10 to finish the regular season 17–10. They lost in the semifinals of the Southeastern Conference Tournament, but first- and second-round victories were enough to secure a fifth consecutive NCAA Tournament invitation.

Assigned to the Mideast Regional for the fourth time in five years, eighth-seeded Tennessee drew ninth-seeded Marquette in the first round. Brooks, whose missed free throws had contributed to Tennessee's NCAA ouster the previous year, hoped for a chance to atone.

He got it. Fouled with 61 seconds left and the score tied at 53, he sank both free throws to give the Big Orange a 2-point lead. Moments later, with Tennessee on top 55–54 and just five seconds on the clock, he coolly sank two more to seal a 57–56 victory.

For the fifth year in a row, Tennessee had notched a first-round triumph in NCAA Tournament play. But, for the fifth year in a row, the Vols would absorb a second-round defeat. Louisville used an 11–2 spurt midway through the second half to turn a 45–43 lead into an eventual 70–57 triumph.

A wistful DeVoe couldn't help wondering what might've been. The Mideast Regional semifinals and finals that year were being held in Knoxville. "If we'd beaten Louisville, we would have come back to Stokely Center to play the Sweet Sixteen," he recalls. "I always felt like if we'd gotten back to Knoxville, we would've reached the Final Four because we were almost unbeatable at home that season."

Despite another second-round NCAA Tournament loss, the coach had plenty of reason to be proud. His first five years on the job had produced five NCAA bids, an SEC regular-season championship (1983), an SEC Tournament championship (1979), four 20-win seasons, and three top-twenty-five rankings.

Two decades later that five-year stretch remains the most successful in Vol history.

The Son Was a Gun

Tied 41–41 with Syracuse barely a minute into the second half on December 9, 1992, the home-standing Tennessee Volunteers desperately needed some points. Quickly getting the ball to their star player, teammates watched intently to see if a basket—and history—would be made.

Freezing a defender with a nifty fake, he squared his shoulders and sprang upward just beyond the three-point line.

Reaching the apex of his jump, he brought his right arm forward, flipped his wrist, and sent the basketball floating goalward. The shot gently swished through the netting—much like hundreds of his shots before it—but this one was different. This one made Allan Houston the leading scorer in Volunteer history.

There was no time to savor the moment, however. Because the game was being nationally televised, play would continue until the next dead-ball situation. When it arrived roughly a minute later, Southeastern Conference official John Clougherty presented the game ball to Tennessee's new scoring leader. As 15,000-plus Vol fans stood and roared their approval, the low-key Houston sheepishly raised his hands in acknowledgement. Then he bounced the record-setting ball toward the Big Orange bench, where it was fielded by Wade Houston, Allan's father and Tennessee's head coach.

Since Wade still had 18:21 of basketball action to oversee, he summoned his offspring to courtside and then whispered in his ear. The obedient son started one way, then the other. Clearly confused, he anxiously searched the crowd for a familiar face. Getting the record-breaking ball to his mom, he discovered, was proving more difficult than getting the milestone had been. "Allan was running around and didn't know what to do," Wade recalled afterward.

"My dad told me, 'Go over there and give the ball to your mom,' but I couldn't find her at first," Allan said. "When I did find her, I gave her a big hug, but I don't think I said anything."

"He didn't," Alice Houston confided.

That was typical, though. Allan Houston let his actions speak for him, and his actions spoke volumes during his four years as a starting guard at Tennessee. He finished his college career as the second-leading scorer in Southeastern Conference history (behind Louisiana State's Pete Maravich) and as the league's all-time leader in three-point baskets. In addition to first place on Tennessee's all-time scoring chart, he left as the school leader in three-point buckets, three-point percentage, field goals made, and free throws made. However his path to greatness would be filled with twists and turns.

Oddly Allan's first brush with basketball didn't involve one. His introduction to hoops didn't involve one of those, either. "When I was young, I used to shoot rolled-up socks through my mom's lamp shades," he recalled. "I'd drive her crazy. I'd try to dunk and tear down the curtain rods."

In an effort to save further damage to the family home, Wade Houston hung a rim about 6 feet above ground on the garage and bought Allen a red, white, and blue basketball. The fact that Allan was barely strong enough to hoist the ball up to the rim didn't stop him from trying . . . and trying . . . and trying. "I was about five or six years old," Allan recalled. "I used to love that little rim."

Shortly thereafter, he was sitting with his mom in the bleachers at Louisville's Male High School, where Wade was the head coach. During a time-out, Alice suddenly realized her son had disappeared. Frantically scanning the gym, she finally spotted him—smack in the middle of his dad's huddle.

Allan hoped to spend his high school years in his dad's huddles, but fate had a different plan. Wade left Male High School to become an assistant at the University of Louisville, where he quickly established a reputation as an ace recruiter. He was on the road scouting other prep players so much, he saw his teenaged son play just six times.

His dad's absence must not have bothered Allan too much, because he developed into one of the country's premier prospects, guiding Ballard High School to a four-year record of 91–13. As his senior year approached, however, college recruiters were nowhere to be found. They assumed he was a lock to join his father at Louisville. They were right. "I never really considered anybody else," Allan recalls. "Just as quickly as it crossed my mind to go somewhere else, that's how quickly it left. I grew up with Louisville basketball."

Indeed. Three times as a youngster he got to experience the excitement of an NCAA Final Four locker room. Twice he was privileged to be there for NCAA championship games.

Signing with Louisville in November of his senior year was a mere formality. He then went out and produced a senior season that had Cardinal fans drooling. He averaged 22.8 points, 7.8 rebounds, and 4.7 assists per game that winter, shooting 54 percent from the field, 53 percent from beyond the three-point arc, and 89 percent from the foul line. A consensus All-American, he projected to be a four-year starter for his hometown university. And that's when his path to greatness took an unexpected turn.

Spring break of 1989 found Allan sitting in the shallow end of a hotel pool, basking in the warm sunlight as tiny ripples of cool water gently lapped against his upper body. Suddenly his peaceful repose was shattered by an approaching intruder. It was his mom, rushing to poolside to share some exciting news. "He got the job!" she gushed. *He* was Wade Houston; *the job* was the head coaching position at Tennessee. Mother and son were ecstatic . . . for maybe five seconds. "She was really excited, and I was really excited," Allan recalls. "Then, a few seconds later, I'm thinking, 'Dang! What am I going to do now?'"

The dilemma was as confounding as it was surprising. He fully assumed his dad would continue to serve as a Louisville aide when he signed scholarship papers with the Cardinals five months earlier. Now the family reunion was off unless . . . "I went into deep thought, because I knew immediately I was going to Tennessee," he says. "I just didn't know how I was going to do it."

The Houstons convinced Louisville head coach Denny Crum to give Allan a release from his letter of intent. That was only half the battle, however. As a transfer, Allan stood to lose his freshman year of eligibility unless the Conference Commissioner's Association would grant a special waiver. "We had an agreement that if I was going to lose a year of eligibility by transferring, I would stay with Louisville," Allan recalls. "But if I could get four years at Tennessee—even if I had to sit out one year first—then it was OK."

Weeks passed. Then months. Though exhausted by the nerve-wracking wait, the family remained faithful and focused. "We all prayed about it," Allan says.

Finally those prayers were answered. Noting special circumstances—"the unity of the Houston family"—the National Letter of Intent Steering Committee agreed to waive the one-year penalty for first-year transfers. The Houstons immediately returned to their knees, this time giving thanks. "I knew it was God's will, because that kind of thing just doesn't happen," Allan says. "I knew He made a provision for us. To get four years with no penalty after you've already signed . . . what a blessing!"

Since every starter was missing from the previous year's team, Tennessee faced a rebuilding season in 1989–90—Allan's freshman year. With five spots to fill, he appeared destined to earn one of them. But which one? His silky-smooth jump shot made him a

Tennessee star Allan Houston and his father/coach Wade Houston.

Honor Thy Father/Coach

Between the ages of five and eighteen, Allan Houston rarely got to see his dad.

From age eighteen through twenty-one, however, he got to make up for lost time.

Wade was Tennessee's head coach, Allan the program's star player. They attended practice together, attended games together, made road trips together, and watched game film together. Along the way they developed a bond few fathers and sons can imagine, let alone achieve. "The best thing about playing for my dad was getting to know him on a level of depth I never would have otherwise," Allan recalls. "I don't think a lot of sons get to know their dad at that level."

Allan has gone on to an outstanding pro career. He even won an Olympic gold medal. However perhaps the most impressive thing he has done since leaving college was to establish a scholarship that is awarded to a deserving Tennessee student each year. "The scholarship," he says, "was my way of trying to reconnect myself with the school and, at the same time, honoring what my father gave to me while I was here."

natural shooting guard. At 6'6", however, he had the size and athleticism to play small forward. Then again, given the Vols' shortage of quality ball handlers, he might be most valuable at point guard.

Ultimately he opened game one as the team's point guard and closed it as the team's hero. His late basket provided the winning points, as Tennessee nipped Austin Peay 71–69 in the Mid-South Classic at Memphis. In addition to his late-game heroics, Houston distinguished himself by leading his team's scoring with 17 points.

He was averaging 11.8 points per game through the first month of the season but turned it up a notch following the Christmas break. He hit 31 points, including a school-record 8 three-pointers, against Fordham. He followed with 22 points against Washington State, 20 against Auburn, 18 against Mississippi State, and 34 against eleventh-ranked Louisiana State.

That five-game stretch saw the lanky Louisvillian average 25 points per game and establish himself as one of the NCAA's premier freshmen. Still, the best was yet to come. In a rematch with Louisiana State, Houston and Tiger superstar Chris Jackson put on a show the likes of which Knoxville had never seen. It was a fireworks display better suited to July the fourth than February the tenth.

Jackson drained an arena-record 10 three-pointers and scored 49 points—the most ever by an opponent at Thompson-Boling Arena. Houston countered with 43 points—the most ever by a Vol in Thompson-Boling and the most ever by a Vol freshman anywhere. Houston also contributed 11 assists and 4 steals, two more career highs. "That's a game I still can't explain," he said years later. "It was like having a career game in three areas [points, assists, steals] my first year here."

Allan Houston became the most prolific scorer in Volunteer history.

Proving that impressive outing was no fluke, Houston came back four days later to score 37 points in a game at Ole Miss.

In spite of these glowing performances, his freshman season was far from idyllic. His father was the first black head coach in Southeastern Conference basketball history, and this subjected him to considerable verbal abuse on foreign courts. "There were a lot of times you could hear things about him and about us as a team," Allan recalls. "It made me angry, and I took it out on the floor. But that's part of it. Dad grew up in that kind of [racially tense] environment, and we knew that was going to happen."

Wade Houston also knew basketball would be overshadowed in football-crazed Knoxville. But he never bothered to share this information with his son. "The big shock for me was coming from Louisville, where basketball is all there is, to Tennessee, where it's kind of the other way around," Allan says. "Dad knew it was going to be a challenge, but it was a shock for me."

This shock didn't stop him from finishing the season with a team-high 20.3 points-per-game average, the second-best freshman scoring mark in school history behind Bernard King's 26.4 average in 1975. Along the way Houston produced 20 or more points sixteen times and 30 or more eight times. For his efforts he was one of two freshmen tabbed first-team All-Southeastern Conference—the other was a 7'1", 280-pound Louisiana State rookie named Shaquille O'Neal.

For a squad that featured five new starters and a new headman, the Volunteers had acquitted themselves quite well in 1989–90. They posted a 10–8 league record, won a first-round game in the National Invitation Tournament, and finished the season 16–14. The future appeared bright. Appearances, of course, can be deceiving.

The early-season loss of senior Greg Bell to academic problems stripped the 1990–91 team of a star-caliber player. Now joined in the starting five by three more sophomores and a seldom-used junior, Houston found himself in an awful predicament: Tennessee's only chance to win most nights was for him to be a ball hog, taking most of the shots and scoring most of the points. It was an unpleasant assignment for an unselfish team player. And it was a recipe for disaster.

After winning five of their first six games, the Volunteers came unglued. Houston produced back-to-back scoring efforts of 37 points (versus Oregon State) and 36 points (versus Wichita State), yet Tennessee lost eight of its next nine. The Vols rallied briefly, winning two of their next three, before dropping eleven of their next twelve to finish regular-season play with an embarrassing 9–21 record and a downright humiliating 3–15 league mark.

The Vols limped into Nashville for the Southeastern Conference Tournament, having lost nineteen of their previous twenty-one games. They viewed the tourney as an opportunity for redemption, but no one gave them a chance to advance . . . including their rivals.

Forced to survive a "play-in" game just to make the eight-team tournament bracket, Tennessee clawed its way past Ole Miss 94–85. The Big Orange came back a night later to shock eighteenth-ranked Mississippi State 87–70. That sent the Cinderella Vols into the tourney semifinals against Georgia, a team that had hammered them by 21 points during the regular season. This was a different day and a different Tennessee team, however. The Vols jumped on top early and romped 85–65. With a couple of minutes remaining, Wade Houston lifted his starters—winners of three games in three days—to give them some rest. Upon reaching the sidelines, Allan wrapped his sweaty arms around his dad's neck and squeezed. "We've finally got something to be happy about," he thought. "We're going to the SEC championship game."

Nationally ranked Alabama beat the weary Vols in the title game the following night, but that didn't matter; Tennessee basketball was no longer a laughingstock.

Grudgingly forced to shoulder most of the scoring burden, Allan had established a school record in 1990–91 with 806 points, shattering the old mark of 724 set eight years earlier by Dale Ellis. Houston's 23.7 points-per-game average ranked second in the Southeastern Conference. He sank 38 consecutive free throws (one shy of the school record), became the second Vol ever to score 1,000 points in two seasons (Bernard King was the first), and nailed 99 shots from three-point range, breaking the school record he had set one year earlier. It was difficult to conceive that his college career still had two years to go.

Having overcome considerable adversity the previous season, the 1991–92 Volunteers scarcely raised an eyebrow when they stumbled to a 1–3 start. Undaunted they rallied to win twelve of their next sixteen games. Three of the victories were especially noteworthy.

The first saw Houston sink a three-point shot with just thirteen seconds left, turning a 76–75 deficit into a 78–76 defeat of Georgia. The second was a 107–85 home-floor blowout of eighth-ranked Kentucky that saw Houston nail 10 of 16 from the field and hit 15 of 16 from the foul line en route to a season-high 36 points. The third was a thrilling 83–81 upset of fifth-ranked Arkansas.

Team chemistry is always an issue when a headman coaches his own son. Charges of preferential treatment surface with alarming ease, especially when the offspring is the team's go-to player and leading scorer. Yet teammates harbored no resentment toward soft-spoken Allan Houston. "Wade is lucky that Allan has talent," Alice Houston once noted. "I think that eliminates a lot of the problems."

Not all of them, though. As the coach's son, Allan recognized that being "just one of the guys" was not an option for him. "As one of the leaders of the team, there was a gap between me and the other players on the team," he said. "Can they really, really talk to you? Can they complain to you? There was always going to be that gap, because the bottom line was that I was the guy scoring most of the points *and* the coach's son. It had to be a tough situation for my teammates, because they could never say to me, 'Man! Coach is crazy.' Because of that, we could never really bond like most teams bond."

Maybe not, but the 1991–92 Vols bonded well enough to win a game in the Southeastern Conference Tournament and earn another bid to the National Invitation Tournament. Getting 33 points from Houston, the Big Orange beat Alabama-Birmingham 71–68 in round one before falling to Virginia in round two. Tennessee's 19–15 record could've been better, but it also could've been worse. Five of the nineteen victories were due to late baskets by the coach's son.

After three standout college seasons, Allan faced an agonizing choice. Clearly he was physically talented enough and emotionally mature enough to play at the next level. The instant riches of the National Basketball Association represented a powerful lure. Still, young Houston felt a strong responsibility to stick around for his senior season of college ball in support of his dad and his Vol teammates.

Knowing his son was agonizing over his go/stay dilemma, Wade Houston took him aside and spoke perhaps the four most

unselfish words any father could ever say: "Don't worry about me." Allan decided shortly thereafter to postpone his pro career for one more year, readily admitting that, "I can honestly say I would've given it more consideration if not for my father."

As his senior season approached, young Houston hoped to go out with a championship. As it was he didn't even go out with a scholarship. Wade Houston was so impressed with flashy LaMarcus Golden, he offered the Memphis prep standout a grant Tennessee didn't have. When Golden accepted, Houston's only option was to take one of his current players off scholarship. He chose his son, even though it would mean digging into his own pocket to pay for Allan's final year of schooling. When a sportswriter pressed the coach on why he would assume this unnecessary financial burden, Wade grinned. "I get a discount," he said, "since I'm on the staff here."

Allan must have inherited his dad's dry wit because he also showed a knack for low-key humor. "Most guys go away to college," he wisecracked. "But me? I took my parents with me."

Already a three-time All-Southeastern Conference selection, Allan added a new distinction when preseason drills began in November of 1992—college basketball's most celebrated walk-on. Naturally he took a lot of good-natured kidding, mostly from his dad. "He always wants to play," Wade deadpanned. "Walk-ons want to come up to you and bug you about playing time."

Allan didn't have to "bug" Wade very often that season. The off-season dismissal of seniors Carlus Groves, Steve Rivers, and Orlando Berry for disciplinary violations left Tennessee with another young and relatively inexperienced team. That placed a

Wade Houston guided Tennessee's program for five seasons.

bigger burden on Allan Houston, who somehow remained oblivious to the pressure. "Whether people realize it or not, this is a lot of fun—just to be here, playing college basketball, to have your face on national TV just for doing something you love to do," he said. "I think a lot of players take that for granted."

Even as the pressures mounted, Allan Houston never cracked. At times it seemed that the greater the pressure, the greater he performed. The Vols, 6–4 and riding a two-game losing streak, limped into Lexington to face second-ranked Kentucky on January 9. The Big Blue alternated three defenders on him, yet Houston sank 9 of 13 goal tries and 12 of 13 free throw attempts en route to a game-high 31 points. Still Kentucky prevailed 84–70.

Senior Dale Brown, one of the three Wildcats who attempted to guard Houston, offered this salute: "He's the best two-guard in the nation. You can't be too high [defensively] or he'll go around you. You can't be too low or he'll shoot over you."

Junior Braddy, another Big Blue defender, seconded that emotion. "If someone with his ability gets the ball, you can't stop him," Braddy said. "To a certain degree, we were trying to contain him, but when he gets off like that, there's nothing you can do."

Following a modest three-game winning streak, Tennessee lost seven of its next eight games. Allan Houston's dream of playing in an NCAA Tournament was fading fast, and even opposing coaches sympathized with the classy young man. "It's unfortunate that Tennessee has struggled because Allan is a credit to our conference," Kentucky's Rick Pitino said. "You'd like to see him go out with a bang."

No doubt Pitino regretted that comment a couple of weeks later. Eight days after guiding the Vols to a 101–91 defeat of number thirteen Arkansas in Fayetteville, Houston scored 27 points in leading Tennessee to a 78–77 upset of Pitino's second-ranked Wildcats, costing them the league title.

How could a Vol team with a losing record play so well on occasion? Even Allan couldn't answer that question. "We're probably the biggest mystery in the nation," he said.

There was no mystery about Allan Houston, though, who proved to be one of the best players in the land. He proved it one more time in his final home appearance for Tennessee, pumping in a season-high 36 points against Georgia. As happened so often, however, his brilliance was not enough to produce a victory. The Vols fell 96–83.

With a 12–16 overall record, Tennessee's only chance to earn a bid to the NCAA Tournament was to win the conference tourney. That didn't happen. Kentucky avenged its earlier loss to the Vols by blasting them 101–40 in the quarterfinal round. His college career ended with a blowout, not an NCAA bid. Yet Allan Houston refused to complain. "So many good things have happened to me down here," he said, "and not going to the Tournament is the only bad one."

Indeed. He scored more points between 1989 and 1993 than any college player in America. He left as the leading scorer in Vol history, the second-leading scorer in Southeastern Conference history, and the number thirteen scorer in NCAA history. For four years he turned Thompson-Boling Arena into his personal stage, giving a virtuoso performance virtually every time. He hit baskets. He grabbed rebounds. He ran the offense. He blocked shots. And somehow, he made everything he did look ridiculously easy.

Except, of course, finding his mom in the stands.

Setting the Table

Following a disastrous four-year stretch that included a pair of school-record twenty-two-loss seasons, the University of Tennessee basketball program called a news conference on March 28, 1994, to introduce its new head coach. The Vols hadn't sniffed an NCAA Tournament bid in eleven years, so the assembled press corps was understandably skeptical.

Fresh from a successful rebuilding job at Marquette, newly hired Kevin O'Neill made a few preliminary remarks and then opened the floor to questions. Eventually one brave soul asked about the difficulty of reviving a Tennessee program that clearly faced some imposing challenges. If he was intent on stunning his audience, O'Neill succeeded: "Jeffrey Dahmer killed and ate seventeen young men five blocks from the Marquette campus," the new coach deadpanned, "and we did pretty good there." And with that one sentence, O'Neill clearly established three things:

1. He would not be politically correct.
2. He would not be subtle.
3. He would not be boring.

O'Neill spent the next three years underscoring these points, enhancing his reputation as a world-class recruiter, and tossing out one-liners with the precise timing of a Rolex. He had all the attributes of a standup comedian except a drummer providing "Ba-da-bum" rim-shots to accentuate his punch lines. For instance:

- He considered holding his initial practice as Tennessee's headman at 12:01 A.M. on October 15, 1994, the first day NCAA regulations permitted, but ultimately set the workout for the afternoon. His explanation? "Our guys don't get in till 3:00 A.M." *Ba-da-bum!*

- Questioned about the players he inherited, he replied, "I've looked at a lot of tapes and, to be honest, I hope I can't tell anything from those tapes." *Ba-da-bum!*

- Noting that he had never seen any of Tennessee's players in action prior to taking the job, he wisecracked, "For me this is like going to a bar and hanging out with ten new friends for a whole year." *Ba-da-bum!*

- Asked how patient he expected Vol fans to be, he responded, "They're with you, win or tie." *Ba-da-bum!*

- When asked why he allowed Chris Brand to rejoin the program after leaving it the previous January, O'Neill replied, "He's the only backcourt player with SEC experience. When he's introduced, at least he'll know which circle on the floor to go stand in. We need that." *Ba-da-bum!*

- Reminded that some good players, including four of the top five scorers from the previous year's team, had left the program, O'Neill answered, "Who said they were good players? They were the guys who scored the most points on a five-win team." *Ba-da-bum!*

O'Neill's quick wit and sharp tongue proved so outrageous that he regularly made headlines in area newspapers and routinely showed up in sound bites on area television stations. The glib and charismatic New Yorker made a few enemies along the way, but he made some friends, too. Most of all he made people remember that Tennessee still had a men's basketball program.

The buzz of excitement grew even louder when the new coach announced plans to do a live radio show following each game—home and away—during which he would field questions from the listening audience. He had used the same ploy back in Milwaukee with mixed results.

Noting the dapper O'Neill's penchant for wearing tailored suits on the sidelines, one Marquette fan grumbled, "Hey, Coach, you know what the problem is? You try to dress too nice.

Kevin O'Neill brought a sharp wit and sharper tongue to the Volunteer sidelines.

You're more worried about dressing than you are about winning." If the comment was blunt, O'Neill's reply was even more so: "You know what you can do? You can kiss my ass."

After relating the story to a sportswriter, O'Neill conceded that such salty language would not fly in conservative East Tennessee. "I realize I'm in the Bible Belt, and I have reformed," he said. "Hail Mary, full of grace, and all that."

With the season opener rapidly approaching, O'Neill made his way to Birmingham for the annual Southeastern Conference Media Days. Normally a mundane affair punctuated by hours of coachspeak and clichés, this year's would be different. O'Neill would see to that.

Noting that he had coached at colleges and high schools throughout the Northern Hemisphere—all prior to his thirty-eighth birthday—the first-year Vol coach noted, "I'm a little like bird do-do; I've been all over the country." *Ba-da-bum!*

Moments later, when asked about comments attributed to him suggesting Kentucky coach Rick Pitino knowingly sent good free-throw shooters to the line in place of guys who actually had been fouled, O'Neill said the fault lay not with Pitino but with the officials. "We should blame them for everything," he quipped. "When in doubt, blame the referees." *Ba-da-bum!*

Weeks later the new coach dazzled the Knoxville Quarterback Club with more well-timed wisecracks. Regarding junior college transfer Damon Johnson, O'Neill said, "He's built like [heavyweight boxer] Mike Tyson. He shoots the ball like Mike Tyson, too." *Ba-da-bum!*

Reminded that Pitino had suggested Wildcat fans purchase the Vols four-game ticket package featuring Kentucky, Georgia, Vanderbilt, and Florida, then sell all but the UK ticket, O'Neill replied, "I think that'd be good because then we'd have all the money, and we wouldn't have them at the other three games." *Ba-da-bum!*

O'Neill's genius for wisecracking and promoting was no surprise to those who knew him well. A brilliant student, he earned his undergraduate degree from Montreal's McGill University, dubbed "The Harvard of Canada." It was during this time that he earned the nickname "Mad Dog"—a testament to his hard-nosed style of play—and developed his enduring respect for the defensive aspect of the game.

He subsequently took his master's degree from Maycrest College in Davenport, Iowa, while guiding the basketball team to an 18–11 record in his first college head-coach job. After a string of stops that included an apprenticeship at Arizona, O'Neill got the head coaching position at Marquette. His last two teams (1993 and 1994) led the NCAA in field goal defense and posted records of 20–8 and 24–9. In an off-the-wall attempt to defend the coach's quirky behavior, Marquette guard Rob Logterman once noted, "I know that Coach gets a bad rap for being a madman, but we all know he's behind us. He just pushes us."

Upon assuming the Tennessee job, O'Neil would push the Vols, too . . . right out the door. He dismissed Ed Gray, the team's leading scorer in 1993–94. He also booted third-leading scorer Shun Sheffield and fifth-leading scorer Cortez Barnes. Fourth-leading scorer LaMarcus Golden left of his own accord, then O'Neill elected not to renew the scholarship of Rodney Bonds, who originally signed with the school as a baseball prospect.

Tennessee's practices lasted three hours and were so intense they seemed to last three days. O'Neill drilled his troops tirelessly and browbeat them mercilessly. He threw profanity-laced tantrums *and* he threw chairs. He allowed just one water break per workout. "We really cherish that one break," 7' center Steve Hamer noted.

One O'Neill tirade was so vile that Hamer couldn't stifle a snicker. Asked what the coach said to trigger such a response, the towering Vol answered, "I don't think it's printable. I don't even think it's sayable."

Tennessee's workouts were so physically and emotionally taxing that Brand quit the team and walked off the floor while one preseason practice was still in progress. Turning to Brand's startled teammates, O'Neill quipped, "Maybe he had a meat loaf in the oven." *Ba-da-bum!*

Jerome Brown bolted shortly thereafter, boosting the defection list to seven. Still those who survived the purge seemed to embrace O'Neill's hard-core approach. "It's a lot more pleasant," star forward Stanley Caldwell said, "because when you play defense as hard as you can and work as hard as he wants you to, you can go home satisfied." Caldwell quit the team six weeks later, boosting the defection total to eight and leaving the Vols with just seven scholarship players.

Responding to complaints that he was running off everyone signed by the previous coaching regime, O'Neill replied, "We could have mollycoddled our way through a lot of things, but where are we going with that? We've got to rebuild a program that's down as far as it's ever been."

Despite the mass exodus from the program, Tennessee made noticeable progress in O'Neill's rookie season. The Vols debuted with a 77–70 exhibition defeat of the Ukraine National Team. Playing stifling defense the Big Orange forced 18 turnovers and limited the visitors to 37 percent field-goal shooting, including an icy 2 of 18 from inside the three-point arc.

It didn't matter that the game was merely an exhibition. Long-suffering Tennessee fans were excited as they phoned in congratulations during O'Neill's postgame call-in show. "We're going to have a pretty good team, aren't we, Coach?" one caller asked. "Yeah," O'Neill replied, "and I may win the lottery." *Ba-da-bum!*

The headman's pessimism was well-founded. The Vols won their first three games, then lost fourteen of their next nineteen. O'Neill may have been at a loss for answers, but he was never at a loss for words. "Going to my bench is like going to the video store late on a Saturday night," he quipped. "There aren't many choices left." The folks at *Sports Illustrated* considered that line so clever they included it in their "They Said It" feature the following week.

An even more printworthy quote might have been the barb O'Neill aimed at the misguided 1993–94 Volunteers of predecessor Wade Houston: "They got on a plane headed for San Juan, and when they landed, they looked out the window and were in Iceland."

O'Neill's first victory was a 74–54 defeat of Tennessee Tech in the regular-season opener. His first Southeastern Conference victory was a 61–57 defeat of South Carolina on January 11. His first SEC road win was a 67–63 squeaker at Vanderbilt. Afterward he showed some nerve by turning to fans behind the Vol bench and raising his arms in celebration. Naturally Commodore supporters were outraged. When told of O'Neill's grandstanding gesture, former Vol coach Ray Mears called it "a hell of an idea," no doubt wishing he'd thought of it first.

Sportswriters loved O'Neill's candor, dubbing him "The Quote Doctor." With the media serving as straight man, the Vol coach elevated the postgame press conference to an art form. While other coaches continued tossing out the same stale platitudes, he was liable to say anything.

Once, asked why forward Kevin Whitted was benched midway through a productive performance, O'Neill replied, "He didn't get much done the first half today, we sat his ass down for a while, then he played pretty well. I think that's the only thing Kevin understands. The quickest message-sender to his brain seems to be his ass."

Another time the coach compared his team to a skirt-chasing bar patron. "Our players try too many difficult passes," he said. "They're like the guy who hits on the prettiest girl in the bar. That's a pass that isn't going to work very often. Your chances are a lot better with the average-looking girl in the corner."

When he wasn't mesmerizing the media with his gift of gab, O'Neill was preaching defense. This emphasis paid immediate dividends. Tennessee ranked second in the conference in scoring defense and third in field-goal defense. The Vols even won three of their last four regular-season games. Still, they trudged into the 1995 Southeastern Conference Tournament with an 11–15 overall record and a 4–12 league mark. Despite losing a ton of games, O'Neill never lost his sense of humor. "We've put a walk-on, Clint Newman, on scholarship," he told reporters covering the tourney. "He works hard in practice and he'll help raise our team GPA [grade-point average]."

Tennessee dropped its tourney opener to finish 11–16, but its rookie coach was undaunted. He knew the key to rebuilding the program was to hit the recruiting trail hard. And no one ever hit it harder than Kevin O'Neill. "If you have good players, you can become a pretty good coach," he explained. "Conversely, if you're a great coach but don't have good players, you're not going to be very good. That's the bottom line."

Voted the nation's best recruiter while an assistant at Arizona in 1989, O'Neill's zest for the task was legendary. During his stint

Gunner Turns Six-Shooter

A four-point possession is rare. A six-point possession is almost unthinkable, especially when one player scores all six points. But that's what happened in a Tennessee–Ole Miss game January 31, 1996, at Knoxville's Thompson-Boling Arena.

Fouled with 1:53 remaining and the Big Orange clinging to a scant 57–51 lead, Vol guard Brandon Wharton was awarded four free throws when the Rebels also incurred a technical foul for overreacting to the call. "I don't think I ever shot four in a row before, so it was kind of weird," the easygoing Wharton said. "I was thinking, 'Golly these are some big free throws,' but I knew I couldn't miss all of 'em."

He didn't miss any of them. Then after draining all four foul shots, he hit a short baseline jump shot. The six-point possession—with all six points scored by Wharton—gave the Volunteers a 63–51 lead. When Tennessee rebounded a missed shot by the visiting Rebels, the Big Orange had a 12-point lead and the ball with less than a minute remaining. They extended the lead in the final minute, ultimately winning 67–52.

Brandon Wharton driving the lane.

TENNESSEE
15
VOLUNTEERS

as a Wildcat aide, he once mailed a prospect thirty-five sticks of chewing gum in thirty-five separate envelopes, each including the note, "Travis, stick with the Wildcats."

One Halloween O'Neill dressed up in a gorilla suit to make a lasting impression on a recruit he was meeting at the airport. Duly impressed, the prospect signed with Arizona.

On another occasion O'Neill was sharing a hotel room with Wildcat head coach Lute Olsen following a hectic day on the recruiting trail. As Olsen slipped under the covers, he noticed O'Neill was still propped up in his bed, busily scribbling notes on the prospects they had visited that day. At midnight Olsen turned his back to the light over O'Neill's head, hoping his aide would take the hint. O'Neill didn't. When Olsen woke up at 2:00 A.M., O'Neill was still scanning his notepad. The head coach dozed off but was awakened a few hours later by a 6:00 A.M. wakeup call. After less than four hours sleep, O'Neill was going jogging. The story doesn't end there, though. "The next day," Olsen recalled, "it was the same thing all over again."

O'Neill's obsession with recruiting did not diminish when he took the reins at Tennessee. If anything the glaring lack of talent he inherited made him even more zealous. Learning that a rival program had told an African-American prospect that the Volunteers were less than hospitable toward minority players, O'Neill immediately telephoned the program's head coach.

After some idle chitchat, O'Neill got to the point of his call. Relating the racially sensitive recruiting incident, he threatened that such slander had better stop immediately or else "I'll kick your ass." When the rival coach sputtered that it was an assistant coach who had made the offending remark, O'Neill snapped, "Then I'll kick his ass, too."

Although a late start limited his first recruiting season at Tennessee, O'Neill reeled in a couple of quality junior college transfers during the spring of 1994. Shane Williams would start every game at guard over the next two seasons and prove to be a defensive whiz. Damon Johnson also would start for two years, proving quite serviceable for a 6'4" forward.

The new coach corralled his first full signing class the following November. Showing he could uncover talent as well as recruit it, O'Neill brought in an unheralded Nashville high schooler named Brandon Wharton. All Wharton did was start for four years and lead the team in scoring three of those seasons.

O'Neill's tireless recruiting efforts kicked into overdrive thereafter. His second full signing class ranked among the top five nationally. The key recruits were 6'10" Charles Hathaway of Nashville, 6'8" C. J. Black of Chattanooga, and 6'9" Isiah Victor of Hopkinsville, Kentucky.

Meanwhile O'Neill was proving to be almost as talented a motivator as he was a recruiter. Before a January 3, 1996 game, Hamer learned that an Auburn radio announcer had described him as a finesse player with a soft work ethic. Enraged, Hamer muscled in eight of eight shots in the second half, finishing with 30 points, 9 rebounds, and 2 blocked shots, as the Volunteers beat the Tigers 66–62. When asked who told Hamer of the Auburn announcer's comment, a smug O'Neill was less than convincing as he replied, "I have absolutely no idea."

Still the youthful Vols would encounter more lows than highs in 1996. They bottomed out in a humiliating late-season loss to Kentucky. Rolling toward a national title, the Big Blue romped 90–50, handing Tennessee the worst home-floor loss in program history. Still O'Neill softened the blow a bit with a witty postgame analogy: "We were like a guy walking through a minefield who steps on every mine."

Even the soft-spoken Hamer offered a touch of sarcasm: "They obviously have more talent than we do, from one through ten, or one through fifteen, or right on down through their managers."

Making the blowout loss to Kentucky even less palatable was the fact two of the Wildcats' premier players were native Tennesseans—Tony Delk (Brownsville) and Ron Mercer (Nashville). O'Neill knew he had to halt this exodus of Volunteer State talent, and that's precisely what he did.

Beating Kentucky for Hathaway was big. Beating Kansas for Black was bigger. Beating the world the following November for heralded Memphis point guard Tony Harris was huge. O'Neill also laid the groundwork for landing the country's top-rated junior prospect, Vincent Yarbrough of Cleveland, Tennessee, by signing his older brother, Del Baker.

Unfortunately O'Neill wasn't having nearly as much success on the basketball floor as he was on the recruiting trail. His second season at the Vol helm ended with a first-round loss in the National Invitation Tournament and a 14–15 overall record. This represented a modest improvement over the previous year's 11–16 mark, but O'Neill suspected the program still had some rough days ahead. He was correct.

Although Victor was approved for eligibility by the NCAA Clearinghouse, school officials ordered him to sit out the 1996–97 season due to concerns about his high school transcript. O'Neill felt betrayed and wasn't shy about saying so. When junior college transfer DeShay Jones suffered a preseason foot injury that plagued him all season, O'Neill was left with a lineup

Steve Hamer had bad knees but a nice shooting touch.

Kevin O'Neill demanded respect from his players—and got it.

consisting of freshmen Hathaway, Black, and Cornelius Jackson, plus sophomores Wharton and Aaron Green.

That much youth and inexperience normally spells trouble in the rugged Southeastern Conference. Sure enough, Tennessee staggered across the finish line with an 11–16 record, matching O'Neill's first season. Still the Vol Nation could hardly wait for the 1997–98 school year. The football outlook was brightened by star quarterback Peyton Manning's decision to return for his senior season rather than jump to the pros. And the basketball outlook was brightened by the return of every key player from 1996–97, plus the availability of blue-chippers Victor and Harris.

But the man who assembled all of this hoops talent would never see it mesh. Five days after Tennessee's 1996–97 season ended with a first-round loss to Auburn in the Southeastern Conference tournament, O'Neill gathered the Volunteers for an impromptu 5:00 A.M. meeting. "You'll be going to the NCAA Tournament next season," he told them, "and you'll be going to the Final Four the year after that." Their coach would not be going with them, however. Instead, Kevin O'Neill—intense, impulsive, but never boring—boarded a plane bound for Chicago, where he would be introduced later that day as the new headman at Northwestern.

Tennessee's players were shocked. So were Tennessee's fans. After three years spent painstakingly assembling the ingredients for a winning team, O'Neill bolted. Essentially he had set the table, only to leave before the meal was served.

Still he went out the same way he came in—cracking wise. "Peyton Manning stayed at Tennessee, and I left," he said. "They got the better of that deal." *Ba-da-bum!*

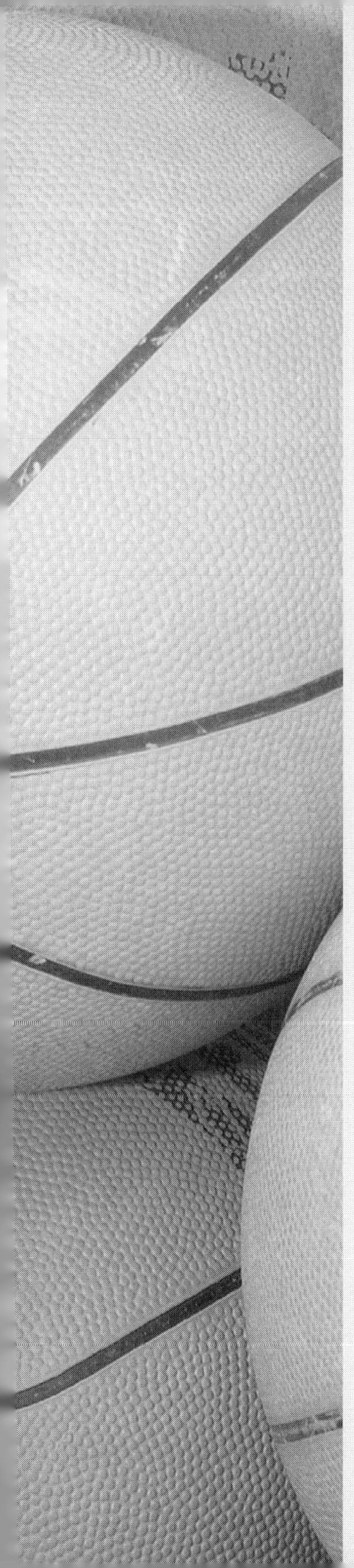

How Sweet It Is!

Every eye at the Frank Erwin Center in Austin, Texas, was trained on Vincent Yarbrough as he stepped to the foul line with 4:48 remaining in the NCAA South Region semifinals March 24, 2000. Taking a deep breath, he focused on the rim 15 feet away and then sent his first free throw sailing toward the basket. It dropped. Another deep breath . . . another long look at the rim . . . another free throw sent hurtling through the tension-filled air. When it, too, dropped, Yarbrough permitted himself a quick glance at the scoreboard: Tennessee 64, North Carolina 57.

A Vol program that had never won more than one game in the NCAA Tournament was in the Sweet Sixteen and fewer than five minutes away from its third win of the 2000 tourney and a berth in the Elite Eight. Clearly the stars were aligned just right. And the stars' names were Yarbrough, Tony Harris, and Isiah Victor. That any of them ended up wearing orange—let alone all three of them—was no small miracle. Just three years earlier, with Tennessee looking for a coach following the abrupt departure of unpredictable Kevin O'Neill, none of the above seemed destined to play for the Volunteers.

Yarbrough, rated the country's number-one prospect heading into his senior year at Cleveland (Tennessee) High School, was leaning heavily to Kentucky. Harris, a slick point guard from Memphis who had signed with Tennessee the previous November, was strongly considering requesting a release from his scholarship now that the man who signed him was gone. "I came real close," Harris admitted. "At one point I felt I wanted to go to Kansas." Victor was so upset by O'Neill's exodus that he began mulling a transfer. "I thought about going to another Division I school," he said. "But I was told to wait and see who we got in as a new coach."

The wait ended, appropriately enough, on April Fool's Day of 1997. Introducing Jerry Green as O'Neill's successor seemed to be some sort of cosmic joke. Born in rural South Carolina, the laid-back Green was Gomer Pyle to O'Neill's Sergeant Carter. Two men could not be more polar opposites. "Anybody they brought in was going to be the opposite of Coach O'Neill," Vol guard

Vincent Yarbrough starting a break to the basket.

Brandon Wharton mused, "unless they brought in Bobby Knight."

Though more akin to Captain Kangaroo than Captain Bly, Green quickly found himself facing the possibility of a mutiny. With several players exploring other options, the new headman sought input from Pat Summitt, coach of the ultrasuccessful Lady Vol basketball program. Her advice, as usual, was blunt: "I don't release anybody," she said.

Slightly modifying Summitt's suggestion, Green called his team together and issued a warning: "If you don't leave now, we won't release you." Two players left. The rest, including Victor, chose to stay. The warning had worked.

Green's next step was to hire ace recruiter Chris Ferguson away from Virginia Tech and assign him the task of swaying Yarbrough. Ferguson succeeded, thanks in part to the fact that Yarbrough's older brother, Del Baker, already was a part of the Vol roster. "I always enjoyed playing with Del," Yarbrough admitted. "That was a big part of my decision to come here."

Re-recruiting Harris was an even greater priority. Green was still mapping his strategy when he got an unsolicited offer from Peyton Manning, Tennessee's All-America quarterback. "Peyton offered to call Tony and lobby on our behalf," Green said. "You can't do that [NCAA rules], but the fact Peyton offered meant so much to me."

With Ferguson bird-dogging Yarbrough, Green assumed personal responsibility for convincing Harris to honor the scholarship he already had signed. Disdaining a truckload of cash, Green showed up in Memphis armed with a video. It wasn't even the XXX-rated variety. This one was rated RRR . . . for run, run, run. The tape showed Green's 1996–97 Oregon Ducks racing up and down the court at breakneck speeds. Harris was hooked. "I was real

Tony Harris led the Vols to four consecutive NCAA Tournament bids.

impressed with that videotape," he said. "When I saw his style of play, I thought, 'This guy can come in and do some things.'" Harris reaffirmed his allegiance to the Vols shortly thereafter.

The basketball gods were smiling on Green, who seemed to be pushing all the right buttons. Still the product he put on the floor would be the ultimate test of his success. His first team, though enormously talented, was generally inexperienced. As a result expectations were a bit unrealistic. Victor was a prime example. Though termed "the best player I ever signed" by O'Neill, he performed erratically as a redshirt freshman in 1997–98. "It was good that he thought I was a good player," Victor said of O'Neill's praise, "but I don't know that I need that added pressure."

While Victor struggled, Harris became an immediate star. The 6' guard proved to be the catalyst in a remarkable one-year turnaround that saw the Vols go from 11–16 to 20–9. Besides leading the team in assists (113), he finished second to Wharton in scoring (14.2 points per game) and steals (36). "I can playmake with the best of them," Harris boasted. "I can do a good job getting everybody else involved."

Green tended to agree. "He's a good shooter, and he's what I call quick on quick," the coach said. "There are guards who are quick and then there are guards who are like jets. I would put Tony in the jet category."

With a year of seasoning behind him, Victor upped his scoring output from 7.7 points per game to 11.3 in 1998–99. Yarbrough cracked the starting lineup two games into his rookie season and contributed 7.6 points per game. With C. J. Black, Victor, and Yarbrough scoring on the inside, Harris and Wharton shot less often but more successfully from the outside. The resulting balance produced a 21–9 record and Tennessee's first East title in the eight years since the Southeastern Conference split into two six-school divisions.

Although Green's first two years featured two 20-win seasons and two NCAA Tournament bids, all indications suggested these were mere preliminaries. Many observers figured the main event would arrive in 1999–2000. That assessment proved correct. The graduation of Wharton was partially offset by the rapid development of freshman guard Jon Higgins, blessed with similar ball-handling and shooting skills. An even greater contribution would come from fellow freshman Ron Slay, a bona fide flake.

In a preview of what was to come, Slay showed up for Tennessee's first practice in a Halloween mask like the one worn by the antagonist in the horror movie *Scream*. The world had been forewarned. Once the season began, Slay played flamboyantly, talked incessantly, and clowned constantly. In short he behaved as if each game amounted to a Harlem Globetrotters audition. The 6'6" forward offered more than comic relief, however. A highly skilled athlete, he provided a tremendous spark in the sixth-man role . . . until Green ordered him to tone down his act. Once Slay's hotdogging was limited, so was his effectiveness.

"Enthusiasm is very important with Ron," Ferguson noted. "I can remember Coach Green talking with Ron about his antics. But when Ron was subdued, he just was not the same player on the court. It affected his game. There's a fine line between being emotional and embarrassing the opponents and the fans, and he needs to get in-between there."

Slay eventually found a happy medium, and so did Tennessee's offense. Showing great versatility and team chemistry, the 1999–2000 Vols swept their first eleven games and

Antics Aside, Slay Could Play

As the 1999–2000 basketball season approached, a dozen Tennessee players gathered at Thompson-Boling Arena for a series of informal "shirts versus skins" pickup games. The "skins" included Ron Slay, a 6'6", 230-pound freshman from Nashville. As Slay removed his shirt, revealing a somewhat soft upper body, Vol freshman Jon Higgins did a double take. "He's got a little weight on him," Higgins recalled. "And the first time I saw him with his shirt off, I'm thinking, 'What's with this guy?'"

Slay showed him moments later, taking an outlet pass and heading up court on a one-man fast break. "He took off from about 2 feet behind the block, went up, and thundered it down," Higgins said, smiling as he recalled the rim-rattling dunk. "He surprised me. I didn't know what to expect from Ron back then, and that continues to this day. You never know what you're going to get."

Wearing his trademark headband, Slay was hard to miss . . . and even harder to stop. He still stands eleventh all-time in career field-goal percentage (49.6) and free throw percentage (75.6).

When that dozen or so Vols gathered for preseason pickup games in 1999, little did they know they were about to embark on a four-year Slay ride.

Ron Slay boxing out for the rebound.

TENNESSE
35

zoomed to number eleven in the national rankings. Following a loss to Tulsa, they won seven of their next eight, improving their record to 18–2. The highlight of this stretch was a double-overtime upset of ninth-ranked Florida in Gainesville.

Although Tennessee finished the regular season with a school-record twenty-four victories and a number eleven ranking, some fans were still skeptical. After all, Green's first two teams had performed well in the regular season only to unravel at tournament time. The 1998 Vols had closed with a second-round loss to Arkansas in the league tournament and a first-round loss to Illinois State in the NCAA Tournament. The 1999 Vols had fared even worse, losing a first-round game to Mississippi State in the conference tourney, then getting annihilated 81–51 by unheralded Southwest Missouri State in round two of the NCAA Tournament.

The skepticism seemed well-founded when the top-seeded Vols lost their opening test to fourth-seeded South Carolina in the league tournament. It wasn't just that the Vols lost but *how* they lost that concerned fans. Leading 68–67 with 4:23 to play, Tennessee missed its last eight shots from the floor. Seven of these were ill-advised three-point tries, and two of them were air balls. Exploiting Tennessee's inexplicable shot selection, the Gamecocks scored the game's final 8 points and won 75–68.

Harris admitted the Vols got "a little rattled," leading fans to wonder if the players were rattled by the league tournament, how could they possibly stay composed in the Big Dance? They wouldn't have to wait long for the answer.

With time running out in round one of the NCAA South Regional at Birmingham, Alabama, Tennessee trailed Louisiana-Lafayette 48–42. Slay came to the rescue at this point, grabbing a defensive rebound and barreling up the floor. Although he resembled a wild bull running through a herd of antelopes, he eventually drove for a layup. Fouled on the shot, his three-point play—ugly though it was—ignited the Vols. "You can't put a saddle on 'em and tell 'em when to go and when not to go," Green said afterward. "You've got to let 'em play. That's what you recruited 'em for."

Slay played, all right. He scored 8 more points in a 15–10 rally that allowed Tennessee to surge ahead 60–58. His all-out effort, coupled with his zany antics, had the Louisiana-Lafayette players befuddled. "Sometimes," Slay said, "they looked at me like I wanted to bite 'em or something."

With 13.3 seconds left, Slay did bite them—figuratively, at least. Harris missed a free throw, but Slay somehow came down with the rebound. Bumped by Lafayette's Lonnie Thomas as he went up for the put-back attempt, Slay crashed awkwardly to the floor, grimacing in pain. He remained there while teammates gathered around and officials assessed the damage. Given the brutality of the assault, the nearest official had little choice but to rule the foul flagrant. This gave Tennessee two free throws plus the next possession, and that proved decisive. Slay missed both free throws but Harris, fouled on the ensuing possession, drained two foul shots to seal the outcome. Higgins added another free throw just before the buzzer to put the lid on a 63–58 Vol victory.

When the final horn sounded, Slay—apparently blessed with miraculous recuperative powers—bounded around the arena in a typically uninhibited celebration. Eventually he stopped long enough to field the question: Was he hurt or was he acting? "Really, I was workin' on my Oscar performance for later this year," he answered, grinning smugly. "I went up strong for the rebound, got pushed in the back, and that's when the Oscar came. . . . The guy kinda kicked one leg out from under me, then I made the other one fly up by myself."

Although Slay and Harris scored 15 points each, Harris said there was no doubt who the game's hero had been. "I think Slay's the main reason we won the game," he said. "Everybody contributed, but Slay really stepped up. He brings everything, and he brought it at the right time."

The dramatic victory earned the Volunteers a berth in the region quarterfinals two days later. Their opponent would be Connecticut—defending national champ Connecticut, that is.

If Tennessee's players were intimidated, they masked it well. The Big Orange closed the first half with a 15–5 run that produced a 32–22 lead. When UConn closed to 38–34 with 13:39 to play, the Vols knew it was time to put up or shut up. They put up.

Higgins nailed a three-pointer, and then Yarbrough added a three-point play on a transition dunk. Black swished a couple of free throws, capping an 8–0 run that widened the gap to 46–34 and drained the life right out of the Huskies. Final score: Tennessee 65, UConn 51. The Vols had shown they could play with the big boys, and they did so in impressive fashion. A balanced attack produced 18 points for Harris, 14 for Yarbrough, and 13 for Black. Moreover the Big Orange recorded 15 assists and just 8 turnovers in what Green called "as good a game as we've played all year."

UConn had no one to blame but itself. The Huskies contributed to their own demise by making some ill-advised comments in the hours leading up to tipoff. "They said we were Pedigree [dog food]," Vol reserve Harris Walker grumbled, "and that they were going to kill us."

Tennessee's players also drew inspiration from a couple of national television "experts" who dared to disrespect them. "We've been watching ESPN all morning," Higgins said. "Digger Phelps and Dick Vitale kept saying they don't think we can win. We got tired of hearing that."

How much the insulting remarks from UConn players and TV announcers helped the Vols is debatable. This much is not: The defeat of the Huskies ranked with the most important triumphs in school history. "This was really a big step for us," Yarbrough said.

Indeed. Prior to beating Connecticut, Tennessee had never won back-to-back NCAA Tournament games in program history. Now the Vols were in the Sweet Sixteen and on the fast track to the Final Four. Though seeded fourth, Tennessee was the highest seed still alive in the South Region. Top-seeded Stanford, second-seeded Cincinnati, and third-seeded Ohio State had fallen victim to early upsets.

The next stop on the road to the Final Four would be Austin, Texas. The opponent would be the North Carolina Tar Heels, one of the most storied programs in NCAA basketball history. Yet with 4:48 remaining, the upstart Volunteers had a 64–57 lead and the confidence that comes from knowing the opponent's best player—7' Brendan Haywood in this case—had fouled out moments earlier.

There would be no Hollywood ending for Tennessee, however. Haywood's departure should've killed Carolina's comeback hopes. Instead it revived them.

Forced to go with an undersized three-guard lineup, Tar Heel coach Bill Guthridge reluctantly switched from man-to-man defense to a matchup zone. This would force the Vols to score from the perimeter.

They couldn't. With the Big Orange unable to find the range, Carolina scored the game's next 13 points, turning the 7-point deficit into a 70–64 lead. By the time the Vols scored again—a Harris 3-pointer with 13.6 seconds left—their fate already was sealed. The final score, 74–69, was not indicative of the performance levels. Tennessee dominated most of the way, only to let the Tar Heels steal the momentum and the game in the waning minutes. "For about thirty-five minutes we played awfully good," Green said. "But the last five minutes we forced shots and didn't move against their zone."

The Vols were understandably disappointed. Victor was especially distraught. "We had it right in our hands," he said. "It's almost like we fumbled."

One week later Tennessee's players gathered around the big-screen television in the team meeting room at Thompson-Boling Arena to watch Florida and Michigan State play for the NCAA championship. It was the same Gator team the Vols had beaten twice during the regular season. Harris summed up the mood in one sentence: "We were thinking, 'This should be us.'"

Eventually, showing the same resilience they had during the season, the Vols bounced back. The hurt healed, and the disappointment faded. By the time they gathered for the postseason awards banquet, they were able to comprehend the magnitude of their achievements.

They posted a 26–7 record, shattering the school record for single-season victories. They won a share of the Southeastern Conference title for the first time in eighteen years. They won six of eight games against nationally ranked opponents. They soared

Isiah Victor leaping high over the basket.

to number five in the national rankings before finishing at number eleven. They advanced deeper into the NCAA Tournament than any team in program history, falling four minutes and forty-eight seconds shy of the Elite Eight. The highlight of the awards banquet arrived when athletics director Doug Dickey eloquently put the season in perspective: "It was a wonderful year. We kept coming back. Every time we went down a little bit, we kept coming back. The clock didn't run out on us; the calendar ran out on us."

About the Author

Randy Moore began covering University of Tennessee basketball in the 1970s, while legendary coach Ray Mears was engaging fans and enraging opponents. Randy's association with the program has continued through the tenures of Don DeVoe, Wade Houston, Kevin O'Neill, Jerry Green, Buzz Peterson, and current headman Bruce Pearl. Having spent much of his thirty-two-year sportswriting career following Vol basketball, Randy has a storehouse of keen insights and colorful anecdotes regarding the program's most amazing athletes and most memorable moments.

THE INSIDER'S SOURCE

With more than 185 South-related titles, we have the area covered. Whether you're looking for the path less traveled, a favorite place to eat, family-friendly fun, a breathtaking hike, or enchanting local attractions, our pages are filled with ideas to get you from one state to the next.

For a complete listing of all our titles, please visit our Web site at www.GlobePequot.com. The Globe Pequot Press is the largest publisher of local travel books in the United States and is a leading source for outdoor recreation guides.

FOR BOOKS TO THE SOUTH

The Globe Pequot Press | INSIDERS' GUIDE® | FALCON GUIDE®

Available wherever books are sold.
Orders can also be placed on the Web at www.GlobePequot.com, by phone from 8:00 A.M. to 5:00 P.M. at 1-800-243-0495, or by fax at 1-800-820-2329.